CAMBRIDGE
Global English

Learner's Book

5

Jane Boylan and Claire Medwell

CAMBRIDGE
UNIVERSITY PRESS

CAMBRIDGE
UNIVERSITY PRESS

University Printing House, Cambridge CB2 8BS, United Kingdom

One Liberty Plaza, 20th Floor, New York, NY 10006, USA

477 Williamstown Road, Port Melbourne, VIC 3207, Australia

314–321, 3rd Floor, Plot 3, Splendor Forum, Jasola District Centre,
New Delhi – 110025, India

103 Penang Road, #05-06/07, Visioncrest Commercial, Singapore 238467

Cambridge University Press is part of the University of Cambridge.

It furthers the University's mission by disseminating knowledge in the pursuit of
education, learning and research at the highest international levels of excellence.

www.cambridge.org
Information on this title: www.cambridge.org/9781107619814

© Cambridge University Press 2014

First published 2014

40 39 38 37 36 35 34 33 32 31 30 29 28 27 26 25 24 23 22

Printed in Poland by Opolgraf

A catalogue record for this publication is available from the British Library

ISBN 978-1-107-61981-4 Learner's Book with Audio CDs (2)

Additional resources for this publication at www.cambridge.org/

Cambridge University Press has no responsibility for the persistence or accuracy
of URLs for external or third-party internet websites referred to in this publication,
and does not guarantee that any content on such websites is, or will remain,
accurate or appropriate. Information regarding prices, travel timetables, and other
factual information given in this work is correct at the time of first printing but
Cambridge University Press does not guarantee the accuracy of such information
thereafter.

Welcome to Cambridge Global English Stage 5

Cambridge Global English is an eight-stage course for learners of English as a Second Language (ESL). The eight stages range from the beginning of primary (Stages 1–6) to the end of the first two years of junior secondary (Stages 7–8). It is ideal for all international ESL learners, and particularly for those following the Cambridge Primary/Secondary English as a Second Language Curriculum Framework, as it has been written to adhere to this framework. It also presents realistic listening and reading texts, writing tasks, and end-of-unit projects similar to those students might encounter in the context of a first-language school. These elements provide teachers with the opportunity to tailor the level of challenge to meet the needs of their particular students. The course is organised into nine thematic units of study which include a range of activities, text types and objectives.

Cambridge Global English materials are aligned with the Common European Framework of Reference. The materials reflect the following principles:

- *An international focus.* Specifically developed for young learners throughout the world, the topics and situations in *Cambridge Global English* have been selected to reflect this diversity and encourage learning about each other's lives through the medium of English.
- *An enquiry-based, language-rich approach to learning. Cambridge Global English* engages children as active, creative learners. At the same time as participating in a range of curriculum-based activities, they can acquire content knowledge, develop critical thinking skills and practise English language and literacy.
- *English for educational success.* To meet the challenges of the future, learners will need to develop facility with both conversational and more formal English. From the earliest stage, *Cambridge Global English* addresses both these competencies. Emphasis is placed on developing the listening, speaking, reading and writing skills learners will need to be successful in using English-language classroom materials.

In addition to this Learner's Book, *Cambridge Global English Activity Book 5* provides supplementary support and practice. Comprehensive support for teachers is available in *Cambridge Global English Teacher's Resource 5*.

The following icons are used in this Learner's Book:

- pre-recorded listening activity
- pairwork or small group speaking activity (not mediated by teacher)
- write in notebook activity
- linking activity in Activity Book
- cross-curricular maths activity
- cross-curricular science activity.

We hope that learners and teachers enjoy using *Cambridge Global English Stage 5* as much as we have enjoyed writing it.

Jane Boylan and Claire Medwell

Contents

Listening/Speaking	School subjects	Phonics / Word study	Critical thinking / Values
Listen for specific information Listen to, prepare, conduct and answer an interview Describe inspirational people	Maths: Calculate dates	Intonation in question forms Rhyming words	Thinking and talking about personal qualities Interpreting attitudes
Evaluate information Listen and plot points on a graph Talk about feeling unwell Do a survey Prepare and give a presentation	Maths: Graphs and charts Science: Health; malaria	Connected speech	Healthy eating – why is it important? Helping each other Completing a table Recognising symptoms Analysing ingredients
Identify opinions Describe places; talk about a story Compare living in the country or city Express opinion Use discourse markers / sequencing words Give presentations: My town and an eco school	Science: Climate change, energy efficiency	-ed endings	Looking after our environment Advantages/disadvantages of urban/rural life Reducing carbon footprint How to make cities cleaner What makes an ideal place to live?
Make connections Listen to descriptions: Celebrations Describe a festival or celebration; talk about personal celebrations Use personal information Give presentations: My coming of age celebration	Maths: 24-hour clock, quantities Comparing	-ough	Understanding and respecting different traditions Interpreting time zones Comparing cultures
Listen to descriptions of famous people Give presentations: A famous person Complete notes: Listen for information Talk about personal achievements Give presentations: A person I admire		Large numbers	Being the best of ourselves Helping others What do we admire in others? Becoming better citizens Recognising personal qualities
Listen to fables Prediction An anecdote Mythical creatures Use connectors when and as Tell an anecdote Discuss a proverb		Stressed and unstressed words	Being courageous Identifying proverbs and myths What can we learn from myths and fables
Listen for clues: Life in ancient Rome Talk about myths, ancient civilisations; the Romans, Talk about different topics Give presentations: Life in your country in ancient times	History: The Egyptians and the Romans Maths: Roman numerals	Identify tone	Being patient Comparing ancient cultures with today
Listen for important information Descriptions of extreme weather Weather reports Give presentations: Practise and present a weather report	Science: Weather	Stress important information Rhyming words	Looking after our world Why are rainforests special? Comparing extreme weather How can we protect our planet?
Listen for specific information: Note-taking Animals and their habitats Look after pets Give advice Give presentations: How to look after a pet	Geography and Science: Animal habitats; the food chain	Rhyming words Alliteration	Researching for a project. Taking care of animals Explaining the food chain Understanding camouflage
Listening/Speaking	School subjects	Phonics / Word study	Critical thinking / Values

5

1 Talking about people

We're going to:

talk about our personalities
do a personality quiz
interview our partners about their lives

write a *My Page* profile
read poems about special people.

1 Talk about it 💬 What are you like?

Think about adjectives to describe yourself.
Give examples.

> I think I'm generous/kind/lazy because ...

2 Vocabulary

Can you find these types of children
in the picture?

> confident   tidy   generous   shy   bad-tempered   hardworking

2 3 Listen

Listen to the speakers describe the children, then use adjectives to describe each child.

Unit 1 Lesson 1 Vocabulary: adjectives to describe personality; antonyms **Listen:** matching **Read:** diary extract **Talk:** discussion

4 [AB] Word study Antonyms

Match the adjectives with their opposite meanings.
Use your dictionary to help you.

1	confident	a	lazy
2	generous	b	cheerful
3	bad-tempered	c	selfish
4	tidy	d	nervous
5	shy	e	untidy
6	hardworking	f	outgoing

5 Read

Read the following extract quickly.
What type of text is it?

Thursday 19th March

Mum has made some new house rules today. She said she's not going to tidy our bedrooms or make our beds anymore. Her three new rules are:

Rule number 1: we have to make our beds every morning.

Rule number 2: we have to put all our clothes away in the wardrobe.

Rule number 3: no toys can be left on the floor and we can only play video games when we have finished tidying up.

I couldn't understand how my little brother Max took only five minutes to tidy his room when it was such a mess. I took 20 minutes to tidy mine. I went to his bedroom and it looked tidy, but when I opened the wardrobe doors all his clothes and toys fell out on top of me. Mum was very angry, and so was I!

6 Talk

Answer the questions about the brothers using adjectives from Activity 4.

1 The writer is called Ben, why is he angry?

2 What is Ben like?

3 Who is Ben's younger brother? What is he like?

4 Do you do chores around the house? If you have any brothers and sisters do they help too?

2 Our profiles

1 Talk about it What do people like about you?

What do you like about yourself? What could you improve about the way you behave?

2 Read Personality quiz

Match the quiz questions A–D with the correct quiz number 1–4.

A You have to read a poem from memory in front of the school. What do you do?

B What do you do if you have an English exam in three days' time?

C How do you behave when you get up in the morning?

D Your friend is unhappy because he/she got low marks in a test. How do you help him/her?

3 Choose the correct answer for you. Read the results at the bottom of the page.

Personality quiz

1

a Start to revise three days before.

b Start to revise a day before.

c Revise during break time before the exam.

2

a You tell your friend not to worry. You're sure his/her marks will improve next term if he/she studies.

b You tell him/her that he/she should have studied harder.

c You tell him/her they deserve bad marks because he/she doesn't hand in his/her homework on time.

3

a You learn it so you can say it from memory and practise in front of a mirror.

b You don't sleep the night before because you think you'll forget the words.

c You go red in the face and feel sick when you get up on the stage.

4

a You sing your favourite song in the shower or as you get dressed.

b You only answer necessary questions from parents, brothers and sisters.

c You don't speak to anyone because you'd prefer to be asleep in your bed.

Results:

Mostly a: You are a cheerful, organised and hardworking person.

Mostly b: Sometimes you are hardworking, but you can study harder and try not to get so nervous before exams.

Mostly c: You are a bit lazy and bad-tempered. You need to study more and be more generous towards your friends.

3 4 Listen

Look carefully at the type of information you need to complete the profile. Listen then copy and complete Santiago's profile. How similar are you to him?

Cool profiles!

Name: Age: Country:

Family: Pets:

Hobbies: Best friends:

What people like about me:

_____

What I like about myself:

_____

What I could improve about myself:

_____

5 Look at the *Use of English* box and use the **Wh-** words to complete these questions. Then answer the questions about Santiago.

1   ... is his name?
2   ... is he from?
3   ... are the people in his family?
4   ... pets has he got?
5   ... are his hobbies?
6   ... are his best friends?
7   ... do people like about him?

Use of English

Question words with **Wh-**
What?   Who?   Where?   When?
Which?   Whose?   Why?

6 Talk

With a partner, ask and answer the questions in Activity 5.

7 Write

Write a profile about your partner. Use the notes you made to help you.

An interview

1 Talk about it 💬 Have you ever had an interview in a foreign language?

How did you feel? What did you talk about?

4 **2 Listen**

Listen to Ben's interview with his new English teacher. Order the topics he talks about.

> family   1
> friends
> favourite things
> town
> personality
> sports
> school

4 **3** 📝 Listen again. Are the sentences **true** or **false**?

1 Ben has got an older brother called Max. False

2 He was born in a small town called Flintown.

3 He is really outgoing.

4 He's known Micky for a long time.

5 He thinks he's good at drawing.

6 He is quite a good rugby player.

7 His favourite things are his video games and comics.

4 Match the questions with the answers.

1 Have you got any brothers or sisters? d   **a** In a small town called Flintown.

2 Where were you born?   **b** I'm quite a confident person.

3 What are you like?   **c** No, not really.

4 Who is your best friend?   **d** Yes, a younger brother called Max.

5 Do you have a favourite sport?   **e** Micky. We've known each other for a long time.

AB **Pronunciation** Intonation in question forms

Listen and write the questions. Can you mark the intonation? Listen again and repeat.

> **1** What are you like?
>
> **2** Do you have a favourite sport?

Speaking tip

Useful expressions for your interview
1 I really like …
2 It makes me (angry)
3 Sorry, could you repeat that?
4 What I meant was …
5 I'm not very keen on …
6 I don't think …
7 We both like …
8 I'm not sure if …

6 Vocabulary

Match the useful expressions in the *Speaking tip* box with the correct category below.

a Checking for meaning 3
b Correcting yourself
c Expressing likes and dislikes
d Comparing
e Expressing opinions

7  **Write**

Prepare questions to ask your partner. Use these prompts to help you.

1 Have / brothers and sisters?
2 Where / born?
3 What / like? (personality)
4 Who / best friends?
5 What / favourite subjects?
6 What / favourite sport?
7 What / favourite things?

An interview

- Prepare your interview. Make notes about your life using the headings below. Use the useful expressions in the *Speaking tip* to describe things you like and don't like.

  My family   My personality   My town   My friends

  My sports   My school   My favourite things

- Use the questions in Activity 7 to interview your partner.
  Then, use your notes to answer questions about your life.

- Don't forget to use the useful expressions in the *Speaking tip*.

4 Favourite things

1 Talk about it
 Look at the girl in the photos. Do you know who she is?

Have you seen the film *Soul Surfer* about her? If not, then read Bethany's story below. How would you describe her?

Bethany's story

Bethany is a professional surfer from Hawaii. At the age of 13, a tiger shark attacked her, biting off her left arm. She was rushed to hospital and despite losing 60% of the blood in her body, she survived. Not only that, but Bethany was determined to surf again and a few months later she was back on her board. In 2004, she wrote about her experience in her autobiography Soul Surfer which was made into a major film in 2011. Today she is a world-class surfer and an inspiration to us all.

2 Read

Read Bethany's *My Page*. Do you have anything in common with her?

Name: Bethany Hamilton

Date of birth: 8th February 1990

Town/City: Lihue, Hawaii

Family: two older brothers, Noah and Timothy

Likes: surfing, playing football, tennis, hiking, rollerblading

Dislikes: having arguments

Personality: cheerful, positive, generous

My perfect day: a warm, sunny day surfing with my friends and family

Favourite things: My most favourite thing of all is my tablet. I've downloaded some amazing apps!

My favourite season: The summer because I love going to the beach. I feel relaxed and happy.

My favourite smell: I love the smell of the sea. It's exhilarating!

My favourite taste: Without a doubt it has to be chocolate!

Advice to others: Do your best in life. Find good in bad situations and be kind to others.

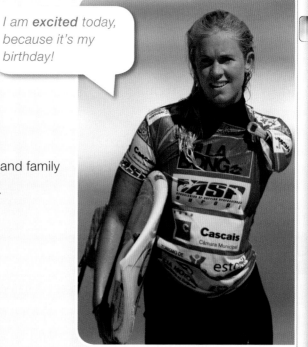

*I am **excited** today, because it's my birthday!*

3 Talk

What's your favourite thing? Your favourite season? Your favourite smell? Your favourite taste? Compare with your partner.

4  **Read**

Find adjectives in the text to describe the nouns below or how people feel about them. Then copy and complete the *Use of English* box.

> the beach   apps   my birthday   the sea

5 **Use of English**

Choose the correct form of the adjectives.

1 I am ___ when I get good results in my English tests because I'm not good at it. (*amazing/amazed*)

2 I am ___ of the dark. I always sleep with a light on at night. (*frightened/frightening*)

3 I think Maths is ___ because I'm not interested in numbers. (*boring/bored*)

4 Surfing is a really ___ sport. (*exciting/excited*)

5 I am ___ when it rains because I can't go outside to play. (*depressing/depressed*)

Use of English

-ed/-ing adjectives

'-ed' adjectives such as ... and ... are used to describe how people feel.

'-ing' adjectives such as ... and ... are used to describe things and situations.

Writing tip

Use different adjectives to make your writing more interesting.

Write Your own *My Page*

• Design the layout of your *My Page*. Find a photo of yourself, and pictures from magazines of your favourite things. Write general information about yourself.

• Write about your favourite things, such as your favourite day of the week. Remember to use **-ed/-ing** adjectives.

• Write about how you feel today and why.

1 Talk about it Discuss with your partner the people who inspire you and why.

6 **2 Listen**

Read and listen to the two poems.
Match a title with each one.

Title 1: **Our teacher's multi-talented** by Kenn Nesbit

Title 2: **Super Samson Simpson** by Jack Prelutsky

Poem A

1 I am _____
I'm **superlatively** strong,
I like to carry elephants,
I do it all day long,
5 I pick up half **a dozen**
and **hoist** them in the air,
it's really somewhat simple,
for I have strength to spare.

My muscles are **enormous**,
10 they bulge from top to toe,
and when I carry elephants,
they ripple to and fro,
but I am not the strongest
in the Simpson family,
15 for when I carry elephants,
my grandma carries me.

Poem B

1 _____
He plays guitar and sings.
He paints impressive pictures
and can juggle twenty rings.

5 He dances like an expert,
he can mambo, tap and waltz.
He's also quite a gymnast,
doing airborne somersaults.

He's something of a swimmer.
10 He's a **champion** at chess.
It's difficult to find a skill
that he does not possess.

He speaks a dozen languages.
He's great at racing cars.
15 He's masterful at fighting bulls,
and studying the stars.

He's good at climbing mountains.
He can **wrestle** with a bear.
The only thing we wish he'd learn
20 is how to comb his hair.

3 Match these illustrations with lines from the poems.

Illustration 1 – Poem A line 2

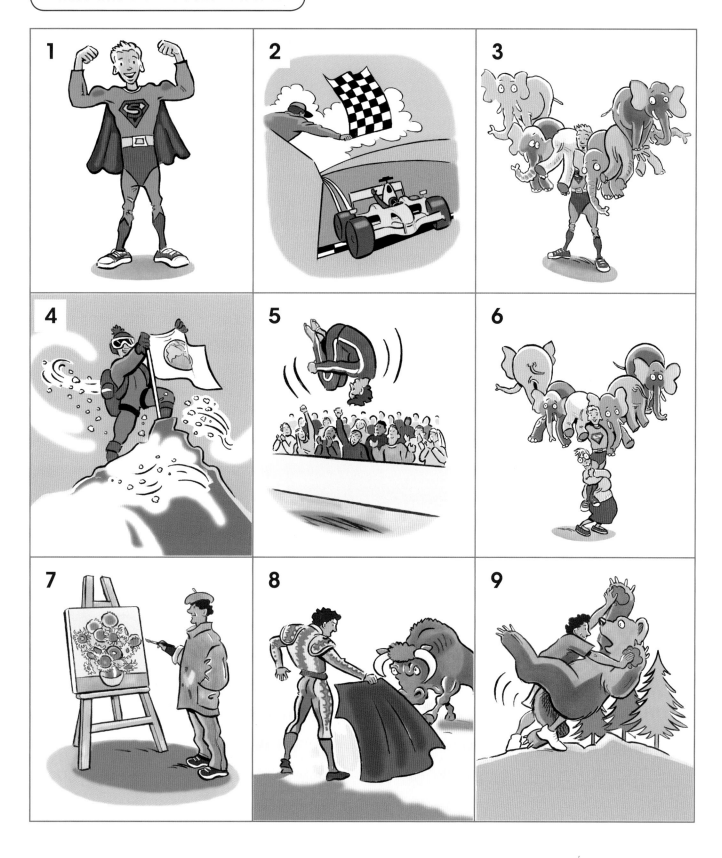

4 📝 Write

Write the following sentences in your notebook and label them **true** or **false**.

1 Super Samson Simpson is good at carrying elephants.
2 His grandma is stronger than he is.
3 The teacher has neat hair.
4 He's very good at chess.
5 He isn't good at swimming.

5 Word study

Match these definitions with the highlighted words in the poems.

1 twelve of something
2 very big
3 a winner of something
4 to fight
5 to lift up
6 extremely

6 Read

Read poem B again on page 14. Find and write the phrases in your notebook that mean 'to be good at something'.

7 Word study

Use your dictionary to find and write definitions for these words.

1 impressive   2 to comb   3 to juggle   4 to carry   5 to bulge   6 an expert

8 💬 Talk

Read out your definitions for your partner to guess.

9 📝 Write Over to you

Think of someone who inspires you then copy and complete these sentences about them.

An inspirational person

He/She can ...

He/She's also quite a ...

He/She's something of a ...

He/She's a champion at ...

He/She's great at ...

He/She's masterful at ...

He/She's good at ...

He/She likes to ...

10 Rhyming words

Match the words that rhyme, then listen and check.

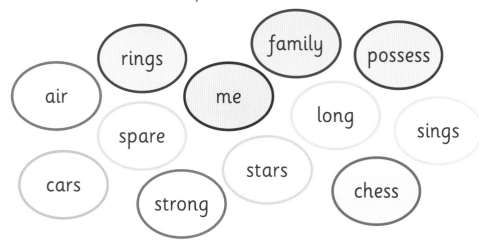

11 Complete the verse about an inspirational person with words from the box, or use your own ideas.

the guitar   three languages   driving cars   archery

She speaks more than … ,
She's good at playing … ,
She likes to …
She's masterful at … ,
And not bad at … .

6 Choose a project

1   My favourite famous person

1   What's the name of your favourite famous person? Where are they from? How old is he or she?

2   What is their profession? What are they famous for?

3   What are they like? Why is he or she your favourite person? Give reasons.

4   Find a picture of your famous person from a magazine or the Internet.

2   The day I was born

1   When is your birthday? What year were you born in?

2   Find out what day of the week you were born on. Ask your parents or tutors or find out on the Internet.

3   Find out how many days you've been alive. Do this by following the instructions below.

   1   Calculate the number of days between the day of your birth and the end of that year.

   2   Calculate the number of days between the start of this year and the date today.

   Note: Remember there are 365 days in a year (apart from leap years when there are 366. Leap years are every four years. The years 2000, 2004 and 2008 were leap years).

   ... days in my first year of life

   + ... × 365 days in the years in between

   + ... extra for leap years

   + ... days of the year up to now

   = ... the number of days you've been alive!

4   Ask your parents or teachers about songs, actors/actresses and films which were popular in the year you were born.

Reflect on your learning

What personal qualities do we like to see in other people?

1 What are the opposites of these adjectives?

bad-tempered   shy   confident   generous   hardworking

2 Write down three adjectives to describe yourself.
Compare with your partner and give reasons.

> I think I'm ... because ...

3 Write six questions to ask your partner about their life using:

What?   Which?   Who?   When?   Where?   Why?

4 Practise the intonation of the questions above.
Remember to use an up-fall intonation.

5 Write down a sound, a smell and a taste that you like.
Compare with your partner.

6 Write sentences using the following adjectives:

bored/boring   relaxed/relaxing   frightened/frightening

7 Write words which rhyme with:

light   day   true   past   bring

L👀k what I can do!

Write or show examples in your notebook.

> **1** I can talk about my life and what I am like.
> **2** I can interview my partner about their life.
> **3** I can write a profile page.
> **4** I can understand a poem.
> **5** I can recognise rhyming words.

2 Staying healthy

We're going to:
talk about common illnesses and their symptoms
read an article about malaria
learn about healthy eating

write a blog entry
read and understand a
world folktale.

1 Talk about it When were you last ill?

Are you ill more in the summer or the winter? How do you feel when you are ill?

2 Word study Common illnesses

Look at the people in the pictures a–f. Which of these illnesses have you had?

3 Match the words with the correct picture.
What illnesses can't you find?
Check their meaning in your dictionary.

> a sore throat   a cold   a cough   earache
> a fever   a headache   stomach ache

4 Listen

Listen to the conversation with a doctor.
Which illness is each speaker suffering from?

8 **5** Listen again and point to the symptoms you hear.

> no energy   lost voice   feel sick   itchy eyes   shivering   head hurts
> runny nose   sweating   tummy hurts   chesty cough   blocked nose

8 **6 Word study** Collocations

Match the words with the correct phrase. Listen again and check.
What words from Activities 3 and 5 can you add?

> a cold   sick   a headache
> dizzy   a sore throat   cold
> stomach ache   a blocked nose

I feel / (s)he feels ...   I've / (s)he's got ...

7 Complete the sentences.
Use **He/She feels** or **He's/She's got**.

1 He ___ a headache.
2 She ___ a sore throat.
3 He ___ a cough.
4 She ___ a cold.
5 She ___ cold.
6 He ___ sick.

8 **Talk**

Point to and talk about the people in the pictures.

> A: What's the matter with her?
> B: She's got a fever. She feels hot.

9 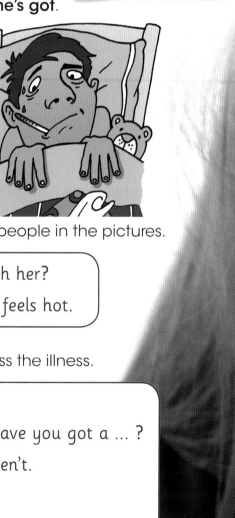 In pairs, mime and guess the illness.

> A: (mime)
> B: What's the matter? Have you got a ... ?
> A: Yes, I have./No, I haven't.
> B: Do you feel ... ?
> A: Yes, I do./No, I don't.

2 Fever

1 Talk about it

A fever is when our body temperature increases because of an infection. A normal body temperature is about 37°C. If you have a fever it can rise to 40°C or more.

1 Have you ever had a fever? **2** How did you feel? **3** How long did it last?

2 💬 Look at the photos below and discuss what you think the text is about.

What is malaria?

Malaria is a very serious disease which infects 300 to 500 million people every year. It is most common in hot tropical countries in the Americas, Asia and Africa. One person dies every second from malaria.

What causes malaria?

A lot of mosquitoes in hot tropical countries carry a parasite which causes malaria. When a mosquito bites a person, the parasite can get into the blood – they don't need to infect **much** blood to make someone very ill.

What are the symptoms?

If you have malaria you will experience **many** symptoms, such as a high fever, headaches and being sick.

How can we stop people getting malaria?

Although there are **plenty of** vaccines which protect us from diseases, there is no vaccine for malaria yet. So all families need to sleep under mosquito nets which are treated with chemicals that make the mosquitoes stay away. For families with **little** money, an organisation called 'Malaria No More' does **a lot of** work to get mosquito nets to them. The nets are so big that **several** people from the same family can sleep under one net. This means that more people can live a healthy life, free from the disease.

3 🔬 **Read**

Read the text. Are sentences 1 to 6 **true** or **false**?

1 Malaria is unusual in hot, tropical countries.

2 Malaria is a deadly disease.

3 Mosquitoes carry a parasite which causes the disease.

4 A high temperature is a symptom of malaria.

5 There are a lot of vaccines which prevent malaria.

6 Mosquito nets help stop malaria infection.

4 📝 🔤 Read the *Use of English* box and sort the words in blue into the correct column.

Countable	Uncountable	Both
a few	much	some
1 ...	any	no
	2 ...	4 ...
	3 ...	5 ...

Reading strategy: Making predictions

Before we read a text we can use visual clues to help us identify what a text is about.

Use of English

Quantifiers

A quantifier expresses quantity.

Countable nouns: There are **a lot of** mosquitoes in hot countries.

Uncountable nouns: For families with **little** money ...

Both: You should drink **plenty of** water when you are ill. / There are **plenty of** vaccines.

All the water is gone.

5 💬 **Talk**

What do you think of the charity Malaria No More?
Do you know of any charities in your country? How do they help?

9 6 📝 **Listen**

Listen, copy and complete the graph showing how Kodjo's temperature rose and fell when he had the flu.

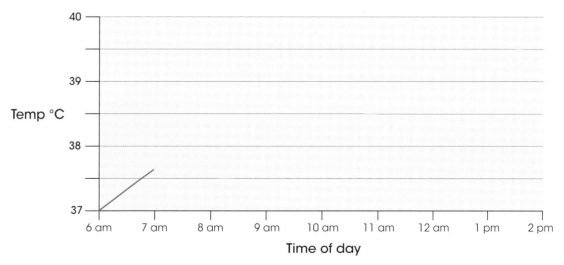

Temp °C

Time of day

3 Food and health

1 Talk about it Do you eat a healthy diet?

What types of foods are healthy and unhealthy?

2 Word study Food groups

Match the food groups with the pictures.

dairy   fruit and vegetables
bad fats and sweets   good fats and oils
grains and cereals   meat and fish

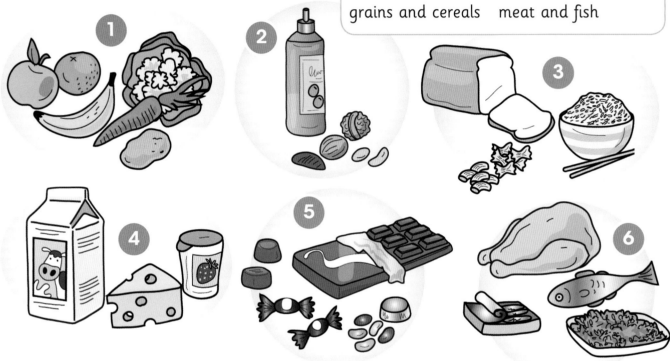

10 3 Listen

Listen to Kaya's presentation on healthy eating. Does she eat healthily?

10 4 Kaya made notes to help her. Listen again and complete her notes in your notebook.

Listening strategy: Evaluating information
Decide what you think about the information you see or hear. Make notes as you listen.

Introduction: Healthy eating is important because ...

Fruit and vegetables give us vitamins and 1 ...
Grains and cereals such as 2 ..., 3 ... and 4 ...
provide our bodies with carbohydrates.
Calcium makes our 5 ... and 6 ... strong.
Some people are vegetarian and so they eat more 7 ...
A lot of sweets harm our 8 ... and ... 9

5 💬 **Talk**

What do you think about the information Kaya gives? Do you agree/disagree?

> I agree. We should eat more fruit and eat less …

10 **6** **Listen**

Listen again to Kaya's advice. Are the sentences **true** or **false**?

1 You should eat fruit and vegetables every day.

2 You shouldn't eat carbohydrates.

3 You should eat yogurt.

4 You should eat pasta and rice because they provide our bodies with proteins.

5 You shouldn't eat meat.

6 You can eat sweets and cakes, but you shouldn't eat them every day.

7  Choose one of these presentation topics. Make short notes on it.

- A healthy school lunch menu
- Healthy birthday party snacks

Use of English

should/shouldn't

You **should** eat fruit as a nutritious snack.

We **shouldn't** eat chocolates and sweets every day.

Speaking tip

Make notes

Make short notes to help you when you are giving a presentation – don't read out your text word for word. Practise your presentation and look at your classmates when you are talking.

Present it!

Healthy eating

- You have been chosen to talk in the school assembly about one of the topics in Activity 7. Use your notes to help you with the presentation.
- Explain why it is important to have a healthy diet.
- Support your presentation with information on the different food groups.
- Explain why you should eat this food. Use verbs of advice.
- Use the *My plate organiser* to help you.

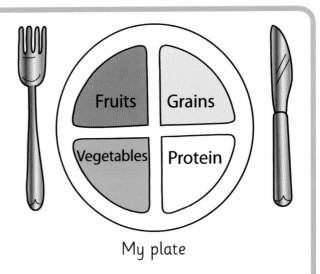

My plate

4 Health blogs

1 Talk about it Why do people go to the doctor?

2 [AB p11] **Word study**

Match the words with the pictures.

> a vaccination   an appointment   an eyesight test
> a hearing test a prescription   a blood test

3 Read and choose the correct answer.

1 I couldn't read the words in the book properly, so mum took me for ___ .

   a a hearing test   **b** an eyesight test

   c a vaccination

2 The doctor recommended ___ to find out if I had an infection.

   a a vaccination   **b** a blood test

   c an appointment

3 My baby brother is only one month old so he has regular ___ .

   a prescriptions   **b** blood tests

   c appointments

4 I had a very bad cough so the doctor gave me ___ for some medicine.

   a an appointment   **b** a prescription

   c an eyesight test

4 Talk

Which of these infections have you had?
Ask your partner. Take turns.

> ear infection   allergic reaction   a skin rash
> a chest infection   a sore throat   a cough

> **A:** Have you ever had a …?
> **B:** Yes, I have. / No, I haven't.

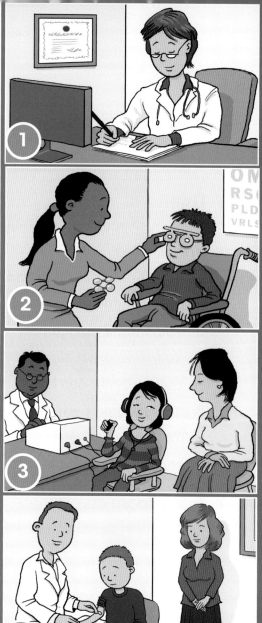

5 Read

Read the text. What kind of text is it? Who do you think the two writers are? Why?

Yesterday, I ate a huge bowl of Mum's homemade tomato soup. It was delicious! However, after an hour or so I got a stomach ache and I started to feel a bit sick. Another hour later, I started to get a red rash on my skin too and it was really itchy. Do you think I could be allergic to tomatoes or could it be something else I ate?

Comment:

It sounds to me like you have a food intolerance. Stop eating tomatoes for a while and see if the symptoms go away. Then try to eat less of them. Although you can probably still eat a slice of tomato in your sandwiches, I'd suggest your mum makes you different kinds of homemade soups in the future. Don't worry you'll probably grow out of this food intolerance. Despite tomatoes being very good for you many people are sensitive to them.

6 Talk

In pairs, talk about the writer's symptoms and the suggestions he is given. Talk about food you like/dislike using contrast linkers.

Although I like tomatoes, I can't eat them.

However, I can eat tomato ketchup!

Write Write a blog entry

- Choose one of the common illnesses from the Unit.
- Write a blog entry explaining the symptoms you have.
- Swap your blog entry with that of your partner.
- Write a diagnosis for your partner's illness and make suggestions using **should/shouldn't**. Remember to contrast information using the linkers.

Writing tip

Contrast linkers

Contrast linkers are used to contrast information.

In spite of and ***despite*** are followed by a gerund (***-ing*** form) or by a noun.

5 Stone soup, a world folktale

1 Talk about it 💬 Look at the ingredients for a soup. Which one is odd?

11 2 Read and listen to the story, then check your answer to Activity 1.

Stone soup

Once there was a young man travelling around the country selling goods. Times were very hard and every day he sold less and less, until he didn't have any money at all. On the same day that he ran out of money and food, he came across a small village. He thought that in the village he would find someone who would give him a bit of food.

He knocked at the door of a pretty-looking house. A woman opened the door slightly. The young man asked the woman if she had a little food to spare for a weary,

young traveller, but sadly the woman answered that she had no food at all. Curiously, the same thing happened at all the houses in the village. There was not even a **crumb of bread** left in the entire village! The young man was not discouraged; instead he came up with a plan.

The young man found a wealthy-looking house in the centre of the village. An elderly man answered the door. The young man asked him if he had a large **pot of water** that he could spare. The old man asked him what he wanted it for. The young man explained that he was so sad about the lack of food in the village that he was going to make a big **pot of soup** for all the villagers from a special stone he had found on his travels.

The old man gave the young man a large pot of water and a stirring spoon and helped him build a big fire next to his house. The young man took a smooth stone out of his bag and put it in the pot of water. As he stirred the water, the young man mentioned to the old man that the magic soup was always better with a little onion and a **head of cabbage** to add extra flavour. So the old man went into his house and returned with a **bag of onions** and a head of cabbage.

A neighbour who was putting out her washing smelled the onions and the cabbage cooking. She went to the old man's house where she was told about the special soup made of stone. The young man who was stirring the soup mentioned that the magic soup was always very good, but that a little bit of meat, perhaps a carrot and some potatoes would add some extra flavour. So the woman went into her house and returned with a **chunk of meat**, a **bunch of carrots** and a **sack of potatoes**.

A little girl who was playing in the street smelled the soup and became curious about the smell. She went to the old man's house. The young man stirred the soup and mentioned to the girl that the magic soup was always very good, but it would be even better with a few beans and a **pinch of salt and pepper**. So, the girl ran into her house and returned with a **bowl of beans** and some salt and pepper and added them to the pot of soup.

The woman from the first house, where the young man had asked for food, was in her garden collecting some herbs and mushrooms. She smelt the soup and became curious about the smell. So, she walked down the lane to the old man's house. The young man stirred the soup some more and mentioned that the magic soup was always very good, but that a few mushrooms and some herbs from her basket would add even more flavour. The woman gladly added her ingredients to the soup.

In a while the soup was cooked and everyone had a bowl of delicious stone soup. No-one could believe that such a flavoursome soup could be made from just a stone. The young man served another bowl of soup and smiled to himself.

3 Read

Answer the questions about the story.

1 Why did the young man decide to make the stone soup?
2 What did the old man give him?
3 What ingredients did the people in the village give him for the stone soup?
4 How did he persuade the people in the village to give him the ingredients for his soup?
5 Why do you think the people in the village wouldn't give him any food when he arrived?
6 Why do you think the young man smiled to himself at the end of the story?
7 What value did the young man teach the people in the village that day?

Vocabulary

goods: things that are transported
weary: tired
discouraged: having lost your confidence
spare: something available because it is extra and not being used
lane: a narrow road in a town or village
flavoursome: food that tastes good

4 📝 Find classifiers for these items from the story. They are in **blue**.

> cabbage   potatoes   salt and pepper
> meat   beans   carrots   onions

12 **5** **Listen**

Listen and repeat the phrases from the story with connected speech.

1   a sack of potatoes
a pot of water
a bunch of carrots
a pinch of salt and pepper
a bowl of beans

2   What happens to *of* ?

3   Is it pronounced differently?

6 **Values** Helping each other

1   How do you help in your home or in your community?

2   Look at the pictures and discuss how these children are helping in their home or community.

7   Make a resolution.

> I'm going to …

Word study: Classifying expressions

We use *of* when we talk about collections of items.

a crumb of bread   **a pot of** water

Pronunciation: Connected speech

We use connected speech to join words together as we speak. This means we often omit sounds or pronounce words differently in order to speak quickly.

6 Choose a project

1 A common illness

Find out about one common illness. Look it up on the Internet or find out more information at the local library.

1 Who is usually affected by this illness? Have you had this illness?

2 What are the symptoms?

3 What should you do if you have this illness?

4 Present your findings to the rest of the class. You could make a poster or do a PowerPoint presentation.

2 A health and food survey

Carry out a health survey with the rest of the pupils in your class to discover how healthy you really are!

1 Ask all your classmates to answer the following questions and write their choices in your notebook. Add some of your own questions too. You could do this in groups, each group being responsible for one of the questions.

1 How often do you eat fruit?

   a never   b twice a week   c three to four times a week   d every day

2 How often do you drink milk?

   a never   b twice a week   c three to four times a week   d every day

3 How often do you eat fish?

   a never   b twice a week   c three to four times a week   d every day

4 How often do you eat chocolates, sweets and cakes?

   a never   b twice a week   c three to four times a week   d every day

2 Present your results for each question in a bar chart and display in the classroom.

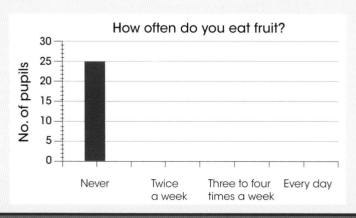

Reflect on your learning

Why is it important to keep healthy?

1 Complete this list of common illnesses: a sore throat ...

2 Write the names of the nutrients our bodies need to keep us healthy.

3 Complete these food collocations.

___ of potatoes

___ of onions

___ of cabbage

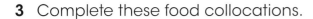

4 Write two more collocations of your own.

5 Write down all the symptoms you can remember for malaria.

6 Write five sentences using these quantifiers.

a few   no   a lot of   much   many

7 Give some health advice to your classmates.

You should eat more fruit.

L👀k what I can do!

Write or show examples in your notebook.

1 I can talk about common illnesses and their symptoms.
2 I can understand an article about malaria.
3 I can give advice on healthy eating.
4 I can write a blog page entry.
5 I can understand a world folktale.

Review 1

13 1 Listen

Listen to the interviews and write in your notebook the information needed to complete the table.

	Name	Age	Family	Likes	Personality
1	Peng				
2					generous
3				surfing	

2 Talk

Interview your partner. Use these prompts to help you.

- What / name?
- Where / from?
- How / old?
- Have / brothers and sisters?
- What / hobbies?
- What / like?

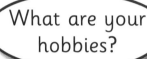

What are your hobbies?

I'm crazy about football.

3 Vocabulary

Read the clues and guess the words.

1 This word describes a person who works very hard.
2 This word describes someone who gets angry a lot.
3 You have this when your head hurts.
4 You have this when you feel hot and shiver.
5 This is a visit to the doctor.
6 This is how you feel when it is your birthday.
7 Our body gets vitamins and minerals from this food group.
8 Yogurt and milk belong to this food group.

4 Use of English

Choose the correct word.

Dear Doctor,

I haven't been feeling very well for (1) *plenty / a few days*.
I feel (2) *headache / dizzy* and (3) *I've got / I feel* a cough.
(4) I *feel / got* hot and cold at night too and I shiver a lot. I'm
drinking (5) *several / a lot* of water. Should I book a doctor's
(6) *vaccination / appointment* or just rest at home?

_____

Dear Patient,

Well it sounds like you (7) *feel / have* got a cold and a
(8) *fever / ear infection* too. You should go to the doctors for
a (9) *blood test / prescription* to buy medicine for your cough
and remember to eat (10) *much / a few* portions of fruit and
vegetables every day. Get (11) *plenty of / many* rest too.

HOME

NEWS

BLOG

5 Read the health blog again and find examples of:

an illness   symptoms   a recommendation

6 Write

Write a diagnosis and make recommendations for a person with the
following symptoms. Remember to use **should** to give advice.

feels sick   stomach ache   no energy

7 Talk

Describe a person who is an inspiration to you. Describe their personality
and the things they are good at. Give reasons for your answer.

3 Where we live

We're going to:

compare the city and the country
read and learn about our carbon footprint
listen to a presentation about a city

talk about the past
write a descriptive essay
read a story

---

1 Talk about it 💬 Do you live in the city or the country? What do you like about it?

2 💬 **Talk**

Look at the photos. Describe what you can see. Talk about the advantages and disadvantages of living in each place.

3 💬 **Word study** Town and country

Use the words from the box to ask questions about the photos.

> **1** Can you see a road?
>
> **2** Yes, here it is.

> road   office buildings   village   vehicle   path
> pavement   lake   forest   mountains   field

14 4 📝 **Listen**

Listen to two children talking about where they live.

1 Which photo is each child describing, A or B?
2 Write a list of the adjectives they use to describe where they live.
3 Which adjective do they both use?

> beautiful   crowded   peaceful   spectacular
> ~~noisy~~   pretty   popular   ~~small~~   modern   ancient

36

Unit 3 Lesson 1 **Vocabulary:** town and country **Use of English:** comparatives and superlatives **Listen:** describing places **Talk:** comparing places **Write:** describing a location

5 (AB) Look at the *Use of English* box and answer the questions.

1 What do we add to short adjectives to make them **a** comparative **b** superlative adjectives?

2 How do we change a short adjective ending in **y** to make it a comparative adjective?

3 How do we make a long adjective with two syllables or more **a** comparative **b** superlative?

6 Talk

Describe the two pictures using adjectives from Activity 4.

> Cork is in the south-west of Ireland, it looks more …

Cork

Dublin

7 Write

Describe and compare the places in the pictures.
Use the map to write about each location.
Use comparatives and superlatives in your description.

> Dublin is in the east of Ireland. It is …

8 Talk

Discuss with your partner which place you would prefer to visit and why.

1 Talk about it   Look at these pictures in the text. What do you

think they represent?

What do you think our carbon footprint is? Why do you think you we need to reduce it?

Reading strategy: Scanning

Read a text or part of a text quickly in order to locate specific information.

2 📖 Read

Scan the text to check if your ideas are correct.

Our carbon footprint

Our carbon footprint is how much CO_2 (Carbon Dioxide) one person makes each year.

What produces carbon dioxide?

We use energy (gas or electricity) every day. Your journey to school, your computer, your mobile phone, the lights and heating in your house – all of these things produce CO_2.

Why are CO_2 emissions a problem?

The problem is that we are all producing too much carbon dioxide and some scientists believe that this is making the Earth hotter. This means the ice at the poles is melting, which will cause sea levels to rise.

How can we reduce our carbon footprint?

There are many things we can do to reduce the energy we use.

- Try walking to school or cycling instead of going by car.
- Recycle materials such as cans, bottles, paper, glass and cartons. This means less energy is needed to make new things.
- Don't leave lights on in your house.
- Eat food which is grown in your area, so planes and lorries aren't needed to transport it from a different country.
- Plant trees in your garden or school as they absorb CO_2 and release oxygen.

3 Are the sentences **true** or **false**?

   1 Our carbon footprint measures the carbon dioxide we produce each year.

   2 Gas and electricity make CO_2.

   3 If you cycle to school you can reduce your carbon footprint.

   4 Trees produce carbon dioxide too.

4 Do the survey. Have you got a big or small carbon footprint? Talk about your answers in pairs.

   1 Do you walk to school?   Yes ○   No ○

   2 Do you recycle materials?   Yes ○   No ○

   3 Do you have a shower instead of bath?   Yes ○   No ○

   4 Do you turn off lights?   Yes ○   No ○

   5 Do you use a computer?   Yes ○   No ○

   6 Do you eat food grown in your garden?   Yes ○   No ○

Conclusion: If you have answered 'yes' to most of these questions then you have a small carbon footprint. Well done!

If you have answered yes to half of the questions then you have a medium-sized carbon footprint.

If you have answered 'no' to most of these questions you have a very big carbon footprint. You need to do something about it!

5 Match the main clause to the correct subordinate clause.

1 I think	**a**	that trees absorb CO_2.
2 I know	**b**	that we should all ride our bikes to school.
3 I hope	**c**	that my generation will reduce global warming.
4 I believe	**d**	that the glaciers don't melt.

6 Talk

Discuss how energy is used at your school. Make a list: *photocopiers, heating*, etc ...

Suggest ways in which your school can reduce its carbon footprint.

> We believe that ... We think that ...

Use of English

Subordinate clauses

These are parts of sentences which need to be connected to the main part to make sense.

... scientists **believe** that this is responsible for rising temperatures on Earth.

1 Talk about it How long have you lived in your town, city or village?

How has it changed? Look at the two photos of London below. What is different?

Listening strategy: Identifying opinions

When you listen to find out the speaker's opinion, listen for words like:

I think …   I (definitely) prefer …   I really like …   In my opinion …

A

B

15 2 Listen to the two parts of Mia's presentation about her city past and present. Which does she prefer, her city in the past or the present?

15 3 Listen again. What vehicles and places are different? Use the words below.

> traffic lights   cars   buses   underground   horse-drawn carriages

> There were no traffic lights in 1910.

4 **Word study** Home appliances

Point to the things you can see in the picture.

> washing machine   microwave
> dishwasher   mobile phone
> television   iron   cooker   fridge

5 Talk

Which home appliances did people use in 1910?

I think that … I'm sure that …

16 6 Listen to the rest of Mia's presentation. Check your answers.

17 7 **Pronunciation** *-ed*

Listen to the pronunciation of the regular verbs. Note them in the correct column in your book.

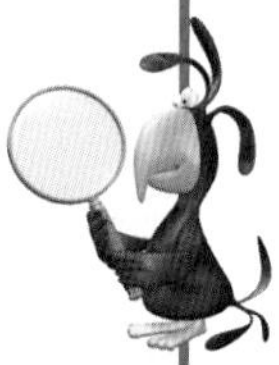

/id/	/t/	/d/
	cooked	

Use of English

Past simple regular and irregular verbs

Regular verbs:

People **cooked** on a stove. (positive)
They **didn't cook** on a stove. (negative)

Irregular verbs:

We don't add ***-ed*** to positive irregular verbs like these in the past simple.
have: had Be: was/were go: went drive: drove ride: rode
My Dad **rode** his bike. (positive)
My Dad **didn't ride** his bike (negative)

Speaking tip

Sequencing words

Use words and phrases to show your listeners where you are in your presentation. This will help you to order your ideas as you present them.

First I'm going to show you photos of … **Then** I'm going to compare …

Next, I'm going to talk about … **Finally, I**'m going to …

Present it!

My town

- Research interesting facts about your town. How has it changed over the last hundred years? Use the Internet or the library. Ask your family.
- Find out how homes have changed in your area and the appliances used in them.
- Divide your presentation into sections as Mia did in her presentation.
- Use photos to compare the past and present. Talk about how life in the home has changed. Give your opinion. Which do you prefer?
- Remember to use comparatives to compare, and the past simple.
- Practise your presentation with a partner.
- Perform your presentation in front of the class.

4 Favourite fictional places

1 Talk about it Think of a book or story you have read recently.

Was it set in a fantasy world or somewhere unusual? Why was it special or unusual?

2 🗨 Talk

Look at the photos below and answer the questions.

1 Have you seen the film or read the books about these places?

2 Which are your favourite places? Why?

3 Think of adjectives to describe these places.

3 📝 Word study Descriptive adjectives

Use the adjectives to describe the places in the pictures.
Use your dictionary to check words you don't know.

> magical   scary-looking   huge   enchanting
> mysterious   colourful   exciting   exotic

4 📝 Use the adjectives in Activity 3 to complete the descriptions.

1 Hogwart's is an enormous, ___ castle.

2 Pandora is an Earth-like moon in the film *Avatar*. It is a ___ place with ___ plants and animals.

3 Neverland is an ___ place because there are battles with pirates.

5 🗨 Talk

Ask your partner which is their favourite fictional place and why?
Try to use the adjectives above. Take turns.

> **A:** Which is your favourite fictional place?
>
> **B:** My favourite place is ... because ...

Hogwart's castle

Pandora

Neverland

6 Read

Read this descriptive essay. Which fictional place is being described?

My favourite fictional place

1 This place is the fifth moon of the planet, Polyphemus. It is smaller than Earth, but more beautiful. It is famous for its beautiful scenery and exotic animals. During the day it looks like a lush, green paradise. At night, the planet life changes colour to blue, purple and green.

2 Some of the animals are magical, like the direhorse, a hexapodal (six-legged horse-like creature) which the Na'vi (the tribes people) ride for hunting. The Na'vi are very tall, two-legged, blue-skinned people. There are very scary animals which live on the planet too, like the viperwolves.

3 I think that this is the most beautiful planet I've ever seen. I'm not very keen on the scary animals, but I would like to meet the Na'vi people and to ride on the direhorse. Also I would like to help the Na'vi defend their planet – humans want to rob precious minerals from the planet because they have used nearly all Earth's natural resources.

7 Answer these questions.

1 Match these headings to the paragraphs **a** Description **b** Opinion **c** Location.

2 Find examples in the text of adjectives used to describe the scenery and the animals.

3 Which expressions does the writer use to express his/her opinions. Find two examples.

📝 **Write** A descriptive essay

• Choose your favourite fictional place.

• Write a list of adjectives to describe this place and its features.

• Write your description. Remember to use paragraphs and check for correct punctuation and good use of adjectives.

• Write about why it is your favourite place. Give your personal opinion.

Writing tip

Use paragraphs

Organise your essay into clear paragraphs: Location, Description, Opinion.

1 Talk about it Have you been on a journey?

Tell your partner where you went, how you got there and what you did.

2 Look at the pictures of a journey. Who are the travellers?
How do they get there? Why do you think they go on this journey?

18 3 Listen and read

Listen and read to check your answers to Activity 2.

The Lost City

1 Yong-Hu and Ho-Shing walked through the valley.

"I'm getting tired," Yong-Hu complained,

"where are we going anyway?"

"We are going to find a city, a lost city.
There are wondrous surprises that await the
ones who find the ancient city."

"Does anyone live there?" Yong-Hu asked.

"Not anymore. At one time it was the busiest city in all of China."

"Why not?"

"Because it is too far out of the way for the trade routes."

"What kind of surprises are there? Good surprises?" Yong-Hu asked.

"Magical surprises," Ho-Shing smiled. "Come."

"Is there **bamboo** in the lost city?" Yong-Hu asked.

"Much."

"Good. Let's hurry up then. I'm starving."

4 Read the first part again. Then read the rest of the text and choose the correct
answer after each section.

   1 The lost city is **a** in a remote location **b** easy to find **c** on a trade route.

   2 The city **a** is not a safe place **b** has many surprises **c** is very busy.

2 After several hours, Ho-Shing stopped. "See the mountains ahead? We are nearly there. Another hour."

Just then they heard a growling sound. "What was that?" Yong-Hu asked.

"A tiger, but it isn't near us. Its **roar** is echoing off the tall mountains."

"There it is! There is the lost city! We have found it at last," Ho-Shing smiled.

"It is magnificent, Ho-Shing. The walls are high and the roofs of the buildings sparkle in the sunshine. Are they made of jade?" Yong-Hu asked.

"There is much **jade**, ivory, gold, silver, and even **rubies**. We must hurry," Ho-Shing said.

"How do we get inside?" Yong-Hu wondered.

"We must climb these steps," Ho-Shing said, pointing to very steep steps that led to the top of the wall.

Yong-Hu laughed and ran up the stairs. After he'd climbed twenty of them he stopped and took a few breaths. "I think I'll walk slowly up the rest of them."

3 Yong-Hu
   a ran up all the steps to the lost city.
   b couldn't climb to the top of the steps.
   c ran up twenty steps and walked the rest.

3 "Ah, there is where we need to go," he said as he reached the top step, "over there, in the middle of the city."

"That is where we shall find our surprises," Ho-Shing said.

They climbed down the steps on the other side of the wall.

"We need to treat this place with respect. Be quiet. Don't touch anything until I say so," he warned his friend.

When they reached the centre of town, a huge, golden gong hung from poles. Several Chinese statues of lions surrounded it. "Look at their ruby eyes!" Yong-Hu said. "Can I bang the gong?" he asked.

"Yes," the wiser panda said.

Yong-Hu picked up the stick and hit the gong.

4 Where do the pandas need to go to find surprises?
 a They need to go down the steps.
 b They need to go to the statue with lions.
 c They need to go to the middle of the city.

4 When the noise stopped, silence filled the air. Crickets began to chirp. "Listen," Ho-Shing said. "It is beautiful."

"When do we get the rubies and jade?" Yong-Hu whispered.

Ho-Shing ignored him and listened to the magical music of the crickets. The two pandas stood silently for an hour, until the crickets stopped singing.

"Our surprise?" Yong-Hu whispered again.

"Yong-Hu, that was our surprise. Nobody in the world has heard anything that beautiful before. It is our reward for our journey," Ho-Shing said.

5 Yong-Hu's surprise was

    a the bamboo   **b** the magical music of the crickets   **c** the rubies and jade.

5 "What about the jade? What about the gold, silver, rubies and ivory?" Yong-Hu asked.

"We cannot touch these things. They belong to the people who once lived in this lost city. You can eat all the bamboo you want, but the rest must stay within these walls," Ho-Shing explained.

At the mention of bamboo, Yong-Hu forgot about all the precious jewels and riches. "Bamboo!" He ran off to search for his feast.

Margo Fallis

5 📝 **Word study**

Match the words in blue in the text with the definitions below.

1 The sound crickets and birds make.

2 A tall, leafy plant that pandas eat.

3 A red precious stone.

4 The sound a lion makes.

5 A green precious stone.

6 A large, circular instrument made of metal or gold.

6 📝 Find the past simple of these verbs in the text.

> walk   hear   find   smile   forget   stand   run   climb   take   arrive

7 Complete these sentences with a verb from Activity 8 in the past simple.

1 They ___ a loud roar.

2 He ___ up the steps to the lost city.

3 Ho-shing laughed as he ___ the stairs.

4 When Yong-Hu saw the bamboo he ___ about the jewels.

5 The two pandas ___ in silence listening to the crickets singing.

8 💬 **Values** Looking after our environment

Why is nobody living in the city in the story?

Where has everybody gone?

If everybody moves from the country to the city to work, the cities will become more crowded and dirty.

Discuss ways in which we can make cities cleaner.

6 Choose a project

1 Design a poster: Our environment

You're going to design a poster on looking after our environment.
The key words are the three *R*s:

Reduce   Recycle   Reuse

1 Brainstorm ways in which we can reduce, recycle and reuse. Make notes. Look back over the unit for ideas.

2 On a large piece of card write the three R words.

3 Decorate your poster by drawing and writing about ways everyone can reduce, recycle and reuse. Use ideas from the unit.

4 Display your poster in the classroom.

2 A presentation: How to become an Eco-school

You're going to prepare a presentation on how your school can become an Eco-school. It can be a presentation for a school assembly or in class.

1 Look back at the notes you made for the discussion on how energy is used in your school on page 39.

2 Add to your list ways in which energy is used at your school.

3 Highlight areas where you think energy could be saved, e.g. lighting.

4 Organise and practise your presentation. Look at pages 24 and 41 again for hints on how to organise your presentation.

5 Give your presentation in front of your class or school. Use your poster or a classmate's poster on looking after the environment for visual help.

Reflect on your learning

Where would be an ideal place to live and why?

1 Write down three adjectives to describe the city, and three to describe the country.

2 Use the comparatives of these adjectives to write four sentences comparing the city and the country.

3 Write true sentences about our carbon footprint using these sentences starters:

> I know that ...   I hope that ...   I think that ...

4 What advice would you give to people who want to reduce their carbon footprint?

5 Tell your partner about your favourite fictional place. Use adjectives from the unit to describe it.

6 Write sentences about the home appliances people didn't use in the early 1900s.

7 Write sentences using these verbs in the past simple.

arrive   wash   go   look   hear   have

LOOk what I can do!

Write or show examples in your notebook.

1 I can compare the city and the country.
2 I can understand an article about our carbon footprint.
3 I can create a presentation about the place I live in.
4 I can talk about the place I live in and what it was like in the past.
5 I can write a descriptive essay.
6 I can understand and talk about the story *The Lost City*.

4 Celebrations

We're going to:
talk about celebrations
read and learn about a celebration
listen to children from different cultures
describing a celebration

talk and write about the future
write an email
read and perform a poem.

1 Talk about it 💬 What celebrations and holidays are important in your family?

Which is your favourite celebration and why?

2 Word study Celebrations

How many of these words can you see in the photos below?
Check the words you don't know in your dictionary.

costumes	fireworks
a feast	decorations
parades	lanterns
symbols	lights	paint

a Holi in India

b Chinese New Year

c May Day

19 3 📝 **Listen**

Listen to a girl describing a celebration.
Which photo above is she describing?
What does she like about it?

4 💬 **Talk**

Which celebration in the photos would
you most like to go to? Why?

5 [AB] [🧪] **Problem solving**

Look at the world clock times on the 24-hour clock and change
to the 12-hour clock time.

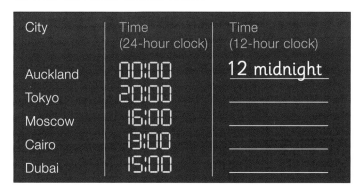

City	Time (24-hour clock)	Time (12-hour clock)
Auckland	00:00	12 midnight
Tokyo	20:00	_____
Moscow	16:00	_____
Cairo	13:00	_____
Dubai	15:00	_____

6 Countries across the world celebrate the New Year at different times.
Read and solve these problems with the help of the clock above.

  1 What time is it in Auckand when Tokyo is celebrating the New Year?

  2 What time is it in Dubai when Cairo is celebrating the New Year?

20 7 [📝] **Listen**

Look at the photos and listen to a description of two different festivals.
Complete the notes below for each one.

  • ____ is celebrated in ____

  • It lasts for ____

  • People decorate/have/go ____

  • The festival celebrates ____

8 [💬] **Talk**

Use the phrases above and vocabulary from Activity 2 to
describe a festival or celebration in your country.

2 The Rio Carnival

1 Talk about it Look at this picture of a celebration.

What can you see? Have you ever been to a celebration like this?

2 Read

Read the information. Check your ideas from Activity 1.

Rio de Janiero in Brazil is famous for its Carnival which is celebrated in February and lasts for four days. The celebration is the world's largest carnival which mixes European traditions with African culture.

There are also thousands of local people who take part in the colourful parades, and tourists who come to watch the carnival too. Everyone joins in the fun of this summer celebration. Samba is a traditional form of Brazilian dance and one of the most important events during the carnival is the Samba School Parade, when neighbourhood groups perform their Samba routines to live music and drummers.

Every year samba schools choose their own theme and create their own carnival floats, spectacular costumes, and music to take part in the Carnival competition. The amazing parade which takes place in the 'Sambódromo' is an avenue specially built for the Carnival and fills the city with the sounds of this fabulous, rhythmic music.

Reading strategy: Visualising a context

When we read a text we create pictures in our minds.
This helps us to understand better what we are reading.

3  **Read**

Read the text again. Close your eyes – what can you see?
Now use the picture in your mind to help you answer the questions.

1 What's the weather like?

2 Are there many people?

3 What are the people in the parade wearing?

4 Describe what the people are doing?

5 What noises can you hear in the carnival?

6 How do you feel watching the carnival?

4 Make a note of the words in the text that helped you form your mind pictures.

Use of English

<u>Defining relative clauses</u>

Defining relative clauses give us important information about a noun or noun phrase. We don't use commas.

We use **who** or **that** to talk about people.

... and tourists **who** *come to watch the carnival too.*

We use **that** or **which** to talk about things.

The amazing parade **which** *takes place in the 'Sambódromo' ...*

5  Look at the *Use of English* box and match the sentence halves.

1 This is the costume

2 People do the Samba

3 I'm going to a Carnival

4 There are thousands of people

a who take part in the parades.

b which I wore in Carnival.

c which is a traditional Brazilian dance.

d that takes place in February.

6 Create it!

You are going to take part in the Carnival. Design the costume you are going to wear and describe it to your classmates.

1 Talk about it What age is special in your family?

Do you have a celebration when you are 18? or at a different age?
What sort of celebration do you have?

> **Listening strategy: Making connections**
> We do this when we compare the information
> we hear with our own lives and culture.

21 · 2 Listen

Listen to children from different cultures talking about 'coming of age'
celebrations. Are any of the celebrations similar to the ones celebrated
in your culture?

21 · 3 📝 Listen again. Match the pictures to the speakers.

Speaker 1 ____ Speaker 2 ____ Speaker 3 ____

a   b   c

21 · 4 📝 Listen again. Copy the table into your notebook and complete it.

Country	A tradition	Age	Special clothes	A feast/special food
Japan				
	Quinceanera			
		21	none	

5 📝 **Word study** Celebrations

Match the verbs to the nouns. You can use some words more than once.

| eat   light   receive | | a song   a blessing   candles |
| get   make   sing | | a cake   food   a gift |

6 Look at the *Use of English* box. Does the form of **will/won't** change?

Use of English

will

We use **will** to express what you believe or know will happen in the future. The contracted form is more common.

I'll (will) **receive** my first kimono.

My mum **will make** a big birthday cake

I **won't have** a big party.

7 📝 [AB] Complete the sentences with the correct verbs and **will**.

wear   receive   celebrate   be   make

1 For the ceremony **I'll wear** a beautiful dress.
2 I ___ my coming of age when I am 20.
3 I ___ gifts from my family and friends.
4 My mum ___ a big birthday cake.
5 It ___ really good fun!

Present it!

My coming of age celebration

• Research facts about your celebration. Ask your parents and your grandparents when it takes place.

• Make notes about the celebration – traditions, costumes, ceremonies, symbols and food.

• Use **will** to express what you believe will happen during the celebration.

• Give your opinion on this celebration. Is it important to you? Why? If not, who is it important for?

Speaking tip

Make it personal
Use information about your own life to make your presentation more personal.

1 Talk about it Do you eat special kinds of food on certain days in the year?

Do you make or buy certain food for special celebrations?
What does it taste like? Do you like it?

Pancake Day

In Britain, Pancake Day (Shrove Tuesday) is celebrated every year in February. On this day, it is traditional to make pancakes, which are thin, flat cakes made out of a mixture of eggs, flour and milk. They are really easy to make and they're **also** delicious with sugar, jam or chocolate on top!

People celebrate with **both** friends and family. It is traditional to 'flip' the pancake which means throwing it into the air and catching it again in your frying pan. Some people have pancake races **as well**! They run as fast as they can to the finishing line whilst flipping the pancake in a pan at the same time!

Other countries celebrate this festival **too**, such as Brazil, Poland and Germany. In France, it's called Mardi Gras which means Fat Tuesday.

Pancake recipe (makes 12–14)
- 110g plain flour
- pinch of salt
- 2 eggs
- 200ml milk mixed with 75ml water
- 50g butter

Mix all the ingredients together **and** then cook a little at a time in hot oil, in a frying pan. Serve them with lemon **and** sugar, jam, chocolate or syrup.

2 💬 🔲 **Talk**

Discuss the questions in pairs.

1 Do you celebrate Pancake Day or a similar festival in your culture?

2 Look at the ingredients – what other flavours or toppings would you add?

3 Can you work out what amount of ingredients you would need to make pancakes for about six people?

Writing tip

 Adding information

Use **both**, **and**, **as well**, **too**, **also**, to add information.

Some people have pancake races **as well / too / ~~both~~**!

People celebrate with **both / ~~as well~~ / ~~also~~** friends and family.

And they're **also / ~~as well~~ / ~~too~~** delicious with sugar.

---

3 Read

Read about the different symbols and choose the correct word.

 The shamrock, or three-leaf clover, is the symbol of Ireland (1) *and / both* the symbol of St Patrick's Day which takes place on 17th March each year. The Irish believe that a four-leaf clover brings good luck (2) *both / too*.

 The dragon is a mythical creature which symbolises power, strength, and good luck. It is (3) *also / too* the luckiest animal in the Chinese zodiac and takes part in New Year celebrations around the world.

 Cornucopia, also known as the 'horn of plenty', is the most common symbol of a harvest festival. It's a horn-shaped container, and it's filled with fruits (4) *also / and* grains. People sometimes put flowers in it (5) *both / as well*.

 Write Describe a celebration

• Choose your favourite celebration.

• Make notes and find out about special food.

• Use your notes to help you write your text.
  Can you write a recipe to go with it?

• Remember to add information using linkers.

• Present your work to your classmates.

1 Talk about it 💬 Do you invite friends to your house?

When do you invite them? What do you do?

22 **2** **Listen and read**

Listen and read the text. What is Horrid Henry organising?

Horrid Henry's Birthday Party

Horrid Henry sat in his fort holding a pad of paper.
On the front cover in big capital letters Henry wrote:
HENRY'S PARTY PLANS – TOP SECRET!!!
At the top of the first page Henry had written:

Guests

A long list followed. Then Henry stared
at the names and chewed his pencil.
Actually, I don't want Margaret, thought
Henry. Too moody. He crossed out
Moody Margaret's name.

And I definitely don't want Susan.
Too crabby.

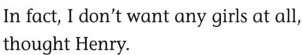

In fact, I don't want any girls at all,
thought Henry.

He crossed out Clever Clare.
And Lazy Linda.

Then there was Anxious Andrew.
Nope, thought Henry, crossing him off.
He's no fun.

Toby was possible, but Henry didn't
really like him. Out went Tough Toby.

William? No way, thought Henry.
He'll be crying the second he gets zapped.
Out went Weepy William.

Ralph? Henry considered. Ralph would
be good because he was sure to get into
trouble. On the other hand, he hadn't
invited Henry to his party. Rude Ralph
was struck off.

So were Babbling Bob, Jolly Josh,
Greedy Graham and Dizzy Dave.

And absolutely no way was Peter
coming anywhere near him on his
birthday. Ahh, that was better.
No horrid kids would be coming to
his party.

There was only one problem. Every single
name was crossed off. No guests meant
no presents.

Francesca Simon

22 **3** 📝 Listen again and answer the questions.

1 How many guests does Henry have on his list to begin with?
2 Who are the first four guests he crosses out on his list?
3 Why does he cross Anxious Andrew off his list?
4 Does he want to invite girls to his party?
5 Why does he cross Ralph off his list?
6 Who do you think Peter is?
7 What is the problem in the end?
8 How do you think Henry feels about this problem?

4 📝 **Word study**

Match the adjectives with the definitions.
Use your dictionary to help you.

1	clever	a	strong
2	moody	b	someone who cries a lot
3	jolly	c	intelligent
4	tough	d	not polite
5	lazy	e	bad-tempered
6	anxious	f	good-humoured
7	weepy	g	not hardworking
8	rude	h	worried/nervous

5 📝 **Antonyms**

Match the opposites. Use your dictionary to help you.

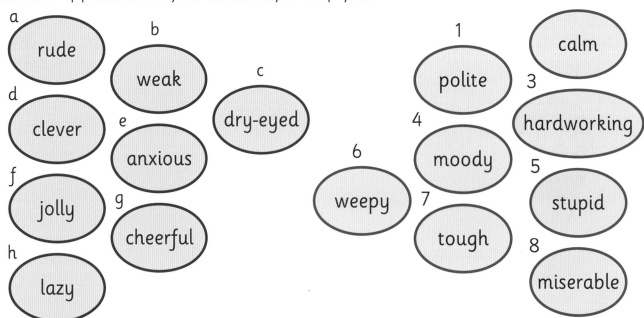

a rude
b weak
c dry-eyed
d clever
e anxious
f jolly
g cheerful
h lazy

1 polite
2 calm
3 hardworking
4 moody
5 stupid
6 weepy
7 tough
8 miserable

6 Read the text again and match the descriptive clues with the children on Henry's guest list.

1   He's always smiling and laughing.
2   She always gets top marks in exams.
3   He doesn't speak nicely to anyone.
4   One minute she's happy, then she's angry.
5   He's so emotional!
6   She never hands in her homework on time.

> Moody Margaret
> Rude Ralph
> Clever Clare
> Lazy Linda
> Weepy William
> Jolly Josh

7 💬 **Talk**

Which of the adjectives would you use to describe yourself? Compare with your partner.

23 8 📝 **Pronunciation** -ough

Listen to the pronunciation of these words. In your notebook group the words which sound the same. **Note:** There are three different sounds.

1   tough   5   rough
2   enough   6   though
3   bought   7   thought
4   dough

9 📝 **Write**

Write a guest list for your birthday. Explain why you want to invite each person. Use positive adjectives to describe each person.

> I'm going to invite Happy Hassan because he will make the party fun.

10 Over to you

Plan a party with a friend. Think about the questions below.

1   Is there a theme to the party (fancy dress, a disco)?
2   What food will you need?
3   What games will you play?
4   How long will it last?
5   Make a poster to advertise your party. Put the poster up around your classroom – look at your classmates' posters, which party would you like to go to? Why?

6 Choose a project

1 Design a poster for a celebration

In groups, you're going to design a poster for a celebration at your school.

1 Decide in your group which celebration you are going to design the poster for (if possible it should be a real celebration which is going to take place at your school).

2 Create a slogan, e.g. "If you like to sing and dance then don't miss our Carnival party!"

3 Include general information: *When? Where? What time? Dress code?*

4 Draw a picture to illustrate the poster, or cut out pictures from magazines.

5 Stick your posters around the school to advertise the celebration.

2 Write an article

You are going to write an article for your school magazine on similarities between different cultures. The topic is festivals and celebrations.

1 Look back over the unit and make a list of the festivals that are similar to those celebrated in your own culture, or that you celebrate too.

2 In your first paragraph, write about festivals that you have in common with other cultures. You could begin by writing *Did you know that … ?*

3 Secondly, write about festivals that have similarities to your own, but also mention the differences. The difference could be the date, a tradition or a symbol. Use addition linkers and contrast linkers.

4 Finally, write your own opinion about similarities between cultures. Were you surprised to find so many similarities? Is there a festival in another culture which you would like to experience? Give reasons why.

Reflect on your learning

Is your culture really that different from others?

1 Write a list of words that are connected to celebrations.

2 Tell your partner how you celebrate New Year with your family.

3 Name all the festivals and celebrations you have learned about in this unit. Select your favourite ones and compare with your partner.

4 Use defining clauses to describe these nouns:

> Samba is a ...   A pancake is a ...
>
> A cornucopia is a ...   A lantern is a ...

5 Write the coming of age celebrations in your culture on a time line.

0 years _____ 100 years

6 Write about when and how you will celebrate them using **will**.

7 Can you remember which celebrations these symbols represent?

LOOk what I can do!

Write or show examples in your notebook.

> 1 I can talk about celebrations in my country.
> 2 I can give a presentation about a 'coming of age' celebration in my culture.
> 3 I can talk and write about the future.
> 4 I can write about a celebration.
> 5 I can understand and perform a poem.

1 ✏️ Vocabulary

in your notebook, label the places with words from the box.

> office buildings   path   underground   mountains
> lake   vehicle   forest   traffic lights   train station

2 ✏️ Use of English

Write sentences comparing the city and the country using the adjectives below.

> noisy   peaceful   clean   crowded   pretty   modern

> The country is quieter than the city.

3 Vocabulary

Read the clues and guess the words.

1 This word describes how much carbon dioxide a person produces in a year.

2 This is an appliance you use to keep food cool.

3 These are things we use to make our houses look pretty for a celebration.

4 You blow these out on a cake when it's your birthday.

5 The term we use for rising temperatures on Earth.

6 An adjective to describe the planet *Pandora*.

7 An adjective which means 'very old'.

4 Listen

Listen and write down the things that **were used** and the things that **weren't used** in the past.

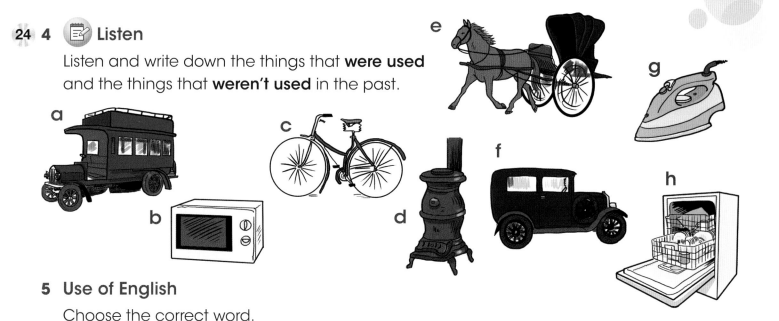

5 Use of English

Choose the correct word.

My last birthday was brilliant. I invited all my school friends to my theme party. The theme was to dress up in a (1) *decoration / costume* of their favourite superhero! Luis (2) *which / who* dressed up as Sonic was the funniest. My mum prepared a delicious (3) *feast / party* of sandwiches, crisps, sweets and soft drinks. She even (4) *did / made* me a Spiderman birthday cake! It's (5) *celebrate / traditional* in my country to make a wish after blowing out the candles on the cake. We (6) *both / also* have a 'pinata', too (7) *which / who* is a special paper bag full of sweets. The birthday child hits the 'pinata' with a stick until all the sweets fall out. We then share them all out. I (8) *received / made* lots of presents from my friends. It was the (9) *worst / best* birthday ever! I don't know how I (10) *won't / will* celebrate my birthday next year – maybe I'll go to the cinema.

6 Write

Write an email to your friend describing how you celebrated your birthday. Use these words to help you.

> eat   receive   sing   celebrate   play   wear

7 Talk

Ask your partner their opinion about life in the future.
Use these prompts to help you.

- flying taxis
- watch phones
- robot teachers
- cars which drive themselves

> Will everyone drive electric cars?
> Yes, I think they will. / No, I think they won't.

5 Famous people

We're going to:

talk about jobs, read about a famous person and their humanitarian work

prepare an interview with a famous person

write a biography

understand an extract from a novel

talk about qualities people have.

1 Talk about it Think of five famous people in your country.

What are their professions?

2 **Word study** Jobs

Can you work out what these people do? Match the professions with the photos.

> artist   explorer   scientist   inventor   entrepreneur   composer

1 Alexander Graham Bell

2 Frida Kahlo

3 Captain Cook

4 JS Bach

5 Marie Curie

6 Steve Jobs

25 3 Listen

Listen and check your answers.

25 4 Listen again. When was each person born and where are they from?

5  **Word study** Personal qualities

Check the meaning of the words below in your dictionary.
What words describe the people in the photos from Activity 2?

> brave   kind   caring   positive   intelligent   determined   fun   creative

6 Look at the *Use of English* box. What form of the verb do we use after the modal verb? Match the sentences that have the same meanings.

1 She can't be a writer.
2 She must be a writer.

a I'm sure she is a writer.
b I'm sure she is not a writer.

> ## Use of English
>
> <u>Modal verbs of speculation</u>
>
> He **could be** a scientist.
> She **might not be** a scientist.

7  **Talk**

Use modals of speculation and the words in the box below to talk about the photos. What jobs do you think they do?

> writer   actress   film director   singer

Michelle Yeoh

Nancy Ajram

Hayao Miyazaki

26 8 **Listen**

Listen and check your answers.
Complete these notes in your notebook.

Name: _____
From: _____
Birth date: _____
Profession: _____
Other information: _____

Arundhati Roy

2 Famous people and their work

1 Talk about it

💬 Can you think of famous people who use their fame to help others?

Who is the person below? How do you think she helps people?

2 Read

Read and check your answers to Activity 1.

1 Shakira is a singer and songwriter. She was born in Colombia in 1977 and is one of Latin America's top pop stars. She speaks fluent Spanish, English, Portuguese and Italian, and reports say she has an IQ of 140, which means she is extremely intelligent! She has sold more than 50 000 000 albums around the world and has won many awards for her work.

2 Shakira began her musical career at an early age. She wrote her first song when she was only eight years old and signed her first record deal with Sony Music in 1990 for three albums. The first two weren't very successful, but the third, released in 1996, *Pies Descalzos* (which means barefoot in English) sold over 5 000 000 copies.

3 At 18, Shakira began her charity work when she set up the Barefoot Foundation to help children in need in Colombia. The Foundation has opened schools and provides children with nutritious meals too. The Foundation has now helped 28 000 children.

She believes that there's more to life than just selling records and she feels she should use her fame to help people with real problems in the real world. She believes that, with time, more and more people will help those in need, making the world a better place.

4 Shakira has eight half-brothers and -sisters. Her father was born in Lebanon, but moved to New York when he was young. Arab music has a great influence on her work. She has a son called Milan who was born in January 2013.

Reading strategy: Matching headings to paragraphs

This helps us to summarise the content of each paragraph and organise our understanding of the text better.

3 Read the text again. Think about what each paragraph is about, then match the headings below with the correct paragraph.

Quick facts   Humanitarian work   Early life and career   Personal life

4 Choose the correct answer.

1 Shakira is ...

  a a songwriter, singer and teacher.

  b a humanitarian worker, a singer and a songwriter.

  c a footballer, a singer and a songwriter.

2 She started her musical career ...

  a when she was 13.

  b when she was very young.

  c when she was ten.

3 Of the three albums she produced ...

  a the first one wasn't very successful, but the third one was.

  b the third was very successful, but the first two weren't.

  c the first and the third albums were the most successful.

4 Shakira has an IQ of 140 which means ...

  a she is quite intelligent.

  b she is more intelligent than anybody else.

  c she is very intelligent.

5 She believes she should ...

  a use her fame to help other people.

  b sell more records.

  c help other people when she sells more records.

27 5 Pronunciation Large numbers

Listen and repeat the numbers.

1 28 000   **2** 50 000 000   **3** 5 000 000   **4** 130 000   **5** 545 000

6 💬 **Talk**

Talk about the questions in groups.

1 What do you think about Shakira? What sort of person is she?

2 Do you know any other famous people who use their fame to help others?

3 A presentation about a famous person

1 Talk about it 💬 Who do you admire and why?

What makes them a special person?

2 💬 Look at the photos. Who are the people and what do you think they do?

28 3 Listen

Listen to the presentations and check your answers to Activity 2.

Listening strategy: Completing notes

- Read the text before listening.
- Think about the missing information: is it a verb, a noun, an adjective … ?
- This will help you as you listen and complete the notes.

28 4 📝 Listen again to the first presentation and complete the notes in your notebook.

I'm going to talk about **1** … Jackie Chan.

He was born on **2** …

When he was very young, he started to **3** … with his father.

At the China Drama Academy, he learned **4** … and acrobatics.

I went to the cinema to see **5** …

5 Read

Read the presentation below about Jane Goodall and replace the words in blue with a more interesting adjective from the box.

> beautiful   remarkable   amazing   exotic   extraordinary

Writing tip

Use different adjectives to make your presentation more interesting.

For my presentation, I am going to talk about Jane Goodall because I think she is a (1) **nice** woman who has led an (2) **nice** life. She was born in London on 3rd April 1934, and lived between London and the (3) **nice** town of Bournemouth, by the sea. When Jane was a child, she liked watching the animals and birds in her garden, but she dreamed of travelling to Africa to observe (4) **nice** animals in their natural habitat. Jane became famous for her (5) **nice** work as an expert on the behaviour of chimpanzees in Tanzania.

28 **6** Listen again to the second presentation and check your answers to Activity 5.

29 **7** [AB] Read the *Use of English* box. Listen and repeat the questions.

1 Jane Goodall is British, **isn't** she?
2 She lived in London, **didn't** she?
3 She dreamed of travelling to Africa, **didn't** she?
4 Jackie Chan's real name means 'born in Hong Kong', **doesn't** it?
5 *The Karate Kid* **was** fantastic, **wasn't** it?

Use of English

Question tags

We use falling intonation when we are checking information we already know.

*Jackie Chan **was** born in China, **wasn't** he?*

Present it!

A famous person I admire

- Research a person you are interested in.
- Make a note of adjectives to describe the person.
- Find pictures to show the class.
- Talk for one or two minutes about him/her.
- Ask three checking questions when your classmate has finished their presentation.

4 A short biography

1 Talk about it Look at the photos below.

What do you know about Felix Baumgartner?
What was the amazing thing he did?

2 Read

Read and check your answers to Activity 1.

My idol: 'Fearless Felix'

1 Have you ever dreamed of going to outer space? Have you ever dreamed of jumping out of a capsule 39 045 metres above Earth? Well, on 14th October 2012, that's just what Felix Baumgartner did!

2 Felix was born in Austria on 20th April 1969. When he was little, he dreamed about flying **and** wanted to be a skydiver when he grew up. When he was five years old he drew a picture for his mum. He was determined to fulfil his dream, **so** he trained to be a skydiver and helicopter pilot.

3 Felix's jump from Earth's stratosphere was the highest and fastest skydive ever! At one point, **because** he was falling so quickly, he began to spin, **but** he soon controlled it. Even though he has jumped from many of the world's highest buildings, Felix spent five years training for the jump, so he knew all the dangers.

4 From my point of view, Felix is incredibly brave and determined, he believes in himself **and** has no fear. I'd like to be a skydiver, like Felix too, one day.

3 Match paragraphs 1 to 4 with the words below.

    a achievements

    b childhood

    c questions to get you thinking

    d the writer's opinion of this person

4 Complete the sentences with one of the conjunctions from the *Writing tip*.

    1 I learned to ride a bike quickly ____ my dad helped me.

    2 My sister studied hard, ____ she got really good marks.

    3 When I passed my piano exam, I was really happy ____ my mum bought me a cake!

    4 I couldn't swim last year, ____ I had some lessons and now I've got my first badge.

> ### Writing tip
> **Conjunctions (1)**
> Use **so**, **and**, **but** and **because** to link parts of sentences in short texts.

5 🗨 [AB] **Talk** Personal achievements

Think of one of your personal achievements. Tell your partner why it was special.

> I got a badge for swimming 50 metres. It was special because I was scared of water before.

6 📝 **Write**

Make notes about people you admire and why. Use adjectives from pages 67 and 71 to describe them.

People I admire	What I admire about them
1	
2	
3	

📝 **Write** A short biography

- Choose someone you admire and make a list of their personal qualities. Use your notes from Activity 6 to help you.
- Divide your ideas into four groups, then write four paragraphs.
- Remember to use conjunctions to link your sentences.

1 Talk about it 💬 Have you ever been on a difficult journey?

Why was it difficult? What do you think a stowaway is?

30 **2** 🔤 **Read and listen**

Read and listen to a summary of the story *The Stowaway* by Karen Hesse.

1 In the summer of 1768, Captain James Cook, a famous explorer, set
sail from England on the HMS *Endeavour* on a three-year journey
to discover an unknown continent on the other side of the world.
Most of the **crew** didn't know that a young boy called Nicholas Young
5 was hiding on the ship. This courageous boy wrote about the perilous
voyage in his journal which he filled with tales of hurricanes, disease,
new lands and strange animals.

31 **3** Now read and listen to Nicholas' diary entries. What is different about the language?
Is it formal or informal? Is it modern or old? How do you know?

4 Read the text again. Are the sentences after each section **true** or **false**?

1

August 1768

Sunday 7th to Friday 19th (Plymouth)

1 With the help of Seamen Francis Haite, John Ramsay and Samuel Evans,
I have managed to keep my presence aboard *Endeavour* a secret. She's a
small **ship**, and her company over 80 in number. It's a wonder I have not
been discovered with all the coming and going of the men aboard, but I
5 have not. The three seamen I paid to get me on bring biscuit and water.
They make certain I exercise each night during middle watch, when there
are fewer hands on deck.

It's a good hiding place I've got, in a small boat *Endeavour* carries aboard
her. I can look over the edge and see the **deck** without being noticed. But
10 it is difficult, lying still, day and night.

1 A young boy called Nicholas was hiding on the ship.

2 Nicholas has some friends on the ship.

3 He can't get up and move around at any time.

2

> *Endeavour* creaks without rest as she sits at **anchor**. The breeze
> chatters her **ropes** against the **masts** and the **ship's bell** clangs
> on the hour and half hour. With all the din of London,
> I thought it could never be so noisy on a ship. But it is.
>
> 15 I've got chickens for neighbours and a goat. They cluck and
> bleat day and night, in pens on the deck. I'm glad of their
> company.
>
> Today, the 19th, Captain Cook gathered the ship's company
> on deck and read the *Articles of War* aloud. Captain is a
> 20 clean-shaven man, strict and stern, with cold eyes.

4 Onboard the ship wasn't as noisy as being in London.

5 There were animals on the deck of the ship.

6 Captain Cook was a friendly man.

3

Sunday 21st (Plymouth)

> We toss at anchor. My stomach heaves and cramps and heaves
> again. And I'm bruised from head to toe. I wish my father would come
> aboard and take me home. I'm tired, wet and hungry. Father knows
> by my letter that I've run out on the Butcher. But I did not write
> 25 where I meant to go, nor what I meant to do, for when I sent the letter,
> I hardly knew my plans myself. Even if he knew, he would not come.
> I am a disappointment to Father. All my brothers are scholars. Only I
> could not settle to my studies. Father has no use for a son who will
> not learn Latin.

7 Nicholas didn't tell his father where he was going.

8 He was different to the rest of his brothers.

4

Wednesday 24th to Thursday 25th (Plymouth)

30 I shall be patient. Father thinks me worthless when it comes to sticking with a plan. He says I run from everything. Well, I did run from Reverend Smythe's school. And from the Butcher. But I had a good cause on both counts. And unhappy as I am, cramped in the hard confines of the boat, I am better off than I was with the Butcher. And so I shall remain,

35 recording my trials in this journal. I shall prove to Father that I am not a quitter. That I am good for something. That I am more than a butcher's boy.

Finally, the rain has stopped. This afternoon, at last, we weighed anchor. Now there are new sounds to join with the others. The wind is clapping

40 the **sails**, the men singing out in the **rigging**, the water churned by *Endeavour's* **prow**. Fine sounds. Sailing sounds.

9 Nicholas ran away from school and the Butcher's where he had a job.

10 Nicholas was determined to prove to his father that he was good at something.

5 Match the old English with the modern English.

1 I shall remain.

2 I could not settle to my studies.

3 Father thinks me worthless.

4 I'm glad of their company.

a I wasn't good at studying.

b I like being with them.

c I will stay.

d My dad doesn't think I'm good at anything.

6 😮 AB **Talk** Class discussion

How would you describe Nicholas?

Why do you think he has decided to stow away on the ship?

7 AB **Read**

Find words in the texts on pages 74–76 to match the meanings below.

From Activity 2

1 brave

2 dangerous

From Activity 4

3 the sounds a chicken and goat make

4 serious

5 a student

6 not worth anything

7 a person who gives up

8  **Word study** Parts of a ship

Find the words in blue in the text and try to work out their meaning. Label the parts of the ship using the words in the box below.

> rigging   anchor   mast   sails   deck   ship's bell   crew   ropes   prow

9 **Talk** Discussion

Would you like to read the rest of this book? Why? Why not?

10 **Values** Showing the best of ourselves

Look at the questions below and discuss them in groups. Use the words in the box to help you.

> independent   brave   determined   foolish   strict   kind   worthless   caring

1 Is it good behaviour to leave home without your parents' permission?

2 In the story, Nicholas wants to show his father that he is good at something. What personal qualities do you think he has shown so far?

3 What qualities do the sailors that help him show?

4 How would you describe your own qualities?

5 What qualities would you like to have that you don't have?

6 Choose a project

1 Special people

1 First organise yourselves into groups of four or five.

2 You need a roll of paper big enough to draw the outline of a volunteer's body on the floor. (If you don't have paper, you can use chalk instead.)

3 Think about a special person in your life. It could be a family member, a friend or someone in your community.

4 Think about why they are special. Think of the personal qualities they have.

5 Each person in the group needs a different coloured pen or piece of chalk.

6 Write the qualities this person has on the outline of the body. Don't write the name of the person.

7 Present this person to the group. Pointing to the personal qualities you have written, as you tell your group why this person is special.

2 A biography

1 Find out about a famous person from your country on the Internet or in the library. When was he/she born? (When did he/she die?) Where is he/she from? Why is he/she famous?

2 Find out about his/her childhood.

3 Find out about his/her achievements.

4 Present your biography to your group or class.

Reflect on your learning

How can we become better citizens?

1 Think of five famous jobs and the name of a famous person as an example for each one.

2 Write four large numbers and ask your partner to say each one. Take turns.

3 Write down three facts you can remember about Jane Goodall. Compare with your partner.

4 Complete each sentence with a question tag.

  1 Shakira is a singer, _____?

  2 Frida Kahlo was a painter, _____?

  3 'Fearless Felix' jumped from Earth's stratosphere, _____?

5 Write five personal qualities.

6 Think of five people who have these qualities, giving reasons why.

> Shakira is caring because she ...

7 Talk about which of these activities you'd like to do or wouldn't like to do. Give reasons.

> skydive   go on a submarine   go on a long sea voyage

LOOk what I can do!

Write or show examples in your notebook.

> 1 I can speak about famous people and their jobs.
>
> 2 I can understand a text about a famous person.
>
> 3 I can give a presentation about a famous person.
>
> 4 I can write a biography of my idol.
>
> 5 I can understand an extract from a novel.
>
> 6 I can talk about personal qualities people have.

⑥ Myths and fables

We're going to:

listen to fables from around the world

describe mythical creatures

tell an anecdote

read and understand simple proverbs

write a short story

read a poem about a mythical creature

---

1 Talk about it 💬 Myths often have fantasy animals as their main characters.

Do you know any myths?

2 Look at the mythical creatures. Match the names with the pictures.
Talk about what you know about them. Were people afraid of them – why?

> Medusa   The Abominable Snowman   Cyclops   The unicorn

32 3 Listen

Listen and check your answers.

4 💬 **Talk**

Which of these mythical creatures do you think
is the most frightening? Which one would you
like to find out more about and why?

5 Read

Find out more about the unicorn and its kindness.
How does it help the animals in this story?

The unicorn who walks alone

The unicorn was a beautiful creature who liked to be alone.

In a land far away there was a wood **where** the animals lived and under the green trees there was a pool of fresh water **where** the animals came to drink. One day a snake slithered out of its cave down to the pool **and** spat his poison into the water.

When the animals walked to the pool to drink they smelt the poison, so they didn't drink the water. They knew they would die **if** they drank from the pool. By evening more and more animals came to the pool. The animals shouted out loud. They were so thirsty! Could anyone help them?

The unicorn who was not far away heard the animals' cries **and** understood that they needed his help, so he galloped faster than the wind to reach the animals. **When** he arrived at the pool he lowered his head and dipped his horn into the water. Then he stood up and told the animals the poison had gone and they could drink the water once again. The animals were so thirsty, they drank and drank. All the animals called out their thanks to the kind unicorn, **but** he had already gone.

6 🗩 Talk

Use the cues to talk about the mythical creatures on this page. Use the conjunctions in brackets.

1 Cyclops / only one eye / see into the future (so)
2 Medusa / meet / goddess Athena / punish her (when)
3 called / Abominable Snowman in the Himalayas / in the American Northwest / called Bigfoot (but)
4 animals thirsty / not drink from the pool (if)
5 snake spit in the pool / animals went to drink (where)

2 Fables

1 Talk about it Fables are short stories which are often about animals.

Can you think of any fables? Which animals are the main characters in the story? What is it about?

> **Reading strategy: Finding specific information in a text**
> Ask yourself what you want to find out before you read a text.

2 Read

Look at the picture and write three questions about information you hope to find.

One summer's day, a happy grasshopper was dancing, singing and playing his violin. He saw an ant passing by, carrying upon his tiny body food to store for the winter.

'Come and sing with me instead of working so hard,' said the grasshopper. 'Let's have fun together.'

'I must store food for the winter,' said the ant, 'and you should do the same.'

'Don't worry about winter, it's still very far away,' said the grasshopper, laughing at him. But the ant wouldn't listen and continued his work.

When the winter came, the starving grasshopper went to the ant's house and begged for something to eat. 'If you had listened to my advice in the summer you would not be hungry now,' said the ant.

3 Talk

Work with a friend and find the answers to your questions.

4 Read

Read the story again and choose which you think is the moral of the story.

a Give your friends food when they are hungry.

b It is best to plan for the future.

c Don't work in the summer.

5 **Listen**

Listen to two fables. Match the titles
with the correct picture.

> **1** *Mat Jambol and the Turtles*
>
> **2** *The Shepherd Boy and the Wolf*

a

b

6 **Talk**

Match one of the morals below with each story. Can you think of other
situations in life where these morals are good?

1 Be responsible   **2** Be honest   **3** Be kind

7 **Word study** Prefixes *un-, ir-, dis-*

Use your dictionary to find out how to make the blue adjectives negative
by adding the correct prefix.

1 The grasshopper was very __**responsible** because he didn't store food for the winter.

2 Mat Jambol didn't want the woman to be __**kind** to the turtles.

3 The shepherd's boy was __**honest**. He lied to the villagers by calling 'wolf!'
when there wasn't one.

8 Match the correct prefix with the words below.

friendly   agree   trust   fair   reliable   regular   like

9 **Talk**

Use the words above to talk about situations in your own life.

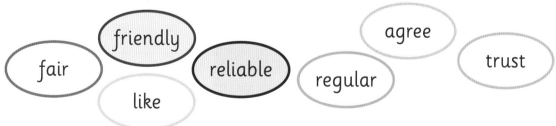

> I often disagree with my sister.
>
> I found some money last week but I was honest and gave it to a teacher.

1 Talk about it Do you remember learning about The Abominable Snowman?
Describe him. Can you remember his different names?

Listening strategy: Prediction

Look at questions or pictures first to guess what words or idea you might hear.

2 Look at the pictures and try to work out the story.
Use the words in the box to help you.

camping   forest   bear   mountain   noise   scared

34 **3 Listen**

Listen to Sophie's anecdote and check your answers.

4 Talk

What other animals live in forests? What do you think the girl saw?

5 [AB] Look at the *Use of English* box. Which verb tells us about an action in progress? Which verb tells us about an action that interrupts the first?

> ## Use of English
>
> <u>Past simple and past continuous</u>
>
> **I was walking** in the mountains *when* **I heard** a noise.
>
> *As* we **were walking** we **saw** something behind a tree.

6 💬 **Talk**

Retell Sophie's anecdote.

- Make notes of words you remember.
- Use the pictures on the opposite page to guide you.
- Use the past simple and past continuous to explain their actions.
- Take it in turns to tell the anecdote.

> ## Speaking tip
>
> [AB] Use the connectors **when** and **as** to connect events that happen at the same time.

Telling an anecdote

- Prepare a short anecdote about something which happened to you. Choose a situation.

  | a holiday adventure | a scary experience | a school trip |

- Write answers to these questions to help you plan your anecdote.

  1 Where were you?

  2 What were you doing?

  3 What happened *first, next, after* and *finally*?

  4 How did you feel?

  5 What was the outcome?

- Tell your anecdote to your group using your answers to the questions above to help you. Remember to use the past continuous and past simple.

1 Talk about it Can you think of any proverbs? What advice do they give?

2 Read

Read this story. What is the missing proverb at the end? Choose **a** or **b**.

a Think before you speak **b** Practice makes perfect

Feathers in the Wind

There was a girl who loved to gossip. Every day she sat at her desk with her friends gossiping about the bad things she thought other people did. 'Can you believe he did that?' 'Can you believe she said that?' 'Did you see what she is wearing?' … on and on she gossiped.

One day her teacher gave her a cushion and told her to go outside, 'Cut it open and throw all the feathers into the wind,' he said.

'Why?' she asked.

'Just do as I say,' said the teacher. The girl went outside and cut open the cushion with a pair of scissors. All the feathers were quickly blown by the wind until they were out of sight.

'Now,' said the teacher. 'I'd like you to go and bring all the feathers back.'

'I can't,' said the girl. 'They have been blown everywhere. I'll never be able to bring them back.'

The teacher looked at the girl. 'And so it is with words and gossip,' he told her. Words once spoken can never be taken back. They can travel far and can do great harm. From now on I want you to _____ . And she did.

3 📝 Read the story again
and complete the Story notes
1–5 in your notebook.

Story notes

1 The story has got two characters: ... , ...
2 The setting is ... .
3 The problem is ... .
4 What happens in order to resolve the problem? ...
5 The resolution is ... .

4 💬 **Word study** Proverbs

Proverbs are very old, wise sayings that give us advice about life.

Look at these proverbs from around the world. Talk about what you think they mean. What would they mean to your own life?

'**Many hands make light work.**'   '*You cannot have a fight alone.*'

'It takes an entire village to raise a child.'

'A man's home is his castle.'   '*A fall in a ditch makes you wiser.*'

'The dog that barks much does not bite.'

📝 **Write** Write a short story

- Write a short story called *A Lesson in Life*. Choose one of the proverbs in Activity 4.
- Think of ideas and makes notes first.
- Decide on your characters. Describe them.
- Where is the story set? Describe the setting.
- Explain the problem and what happens in order to resolve it.
- How does the story end? What is the resolution?
- Remember to use direct speech and useful story expressions.
- Read your story to your partner – can they guess which proverb it matches?

Writing tip

AB **Punctuation** Direct speech

Use direct speech in a story to make it sound more real. Look at how direct speech is punctuated in the story.

'Can you believe he did that**?**' she said. 'I can't**,**' said the girl.

- We use speech marks (' ') at the beginning and the end of the sentence.
- Question marks (?) commas (,) and exclamation marks (!) go inside the speech marks.

1 Talk about it 💬 This is a poem about a monstrous worm which killed animals and ate children. Are there any legends in your country about monstrous animals?

35 2 Listen and read

Read and listen to the poem. Match the pictures with the correct verse.

The Lambton Worm

One morning John Lambton was fishing
In the River Wear.
He caught a fish upon his hook
And gave a little cheer.
Just what kind of fish it was
Young Lambton could not tell
He couldn't be bothered to carry it home
So he threw it down a well.

Now Lambton thought he would like to be
A soldier, and fight in wars.
He joined a group of knights so *tough*
They didn't mind wounds or scars.
They travelled far and had adventures
Lots of stories he could tell.
Very soon he forgot about
The strange thing in the well.

But the worm got fat and grew and grew
And grew an *awful* size.
It had great big teeth, a great big mouth,
And great big goggly eyes.
And when at night it crawled about
Having a little *browse*
If it felt thirsty on the way
It milked a dozen cows.

a

b

c

This *scary* worm would often feed
On calves and lambs and sheep.
And swallow little kids alive
When they were *fast asleep*.
And when it had eaten all it could
And it had had its fill
It crawled away and wrapped itself
Ten times round Penshaw Hill

The news of this awful worm
And its strange goings on
Soon crossed the seas, and got to the ears
Of *brave* and bold Sir John.
So home he came and caught the beast
And cut it in two halves
And that soon stopped it eating kids
And sheep and lambs and calves.

So now you know how everyone
On both sides of the Wear
Lost lots of sheep and lots of sleep
And lived in mortal fear.
So let's say thanks to brave Sir John
Who kept the kids from *harm*
Saved cows and calves by making halves
Of the famous Lambton Worm.

35

3 Listen and read

Listen again and complete a summary of the poem with the correct verb in the past simple or past continuous.

One day when John Lambton **1** … (*fish*) he caught a strange fish, so he **2** … (*throw*) it in the well. Some time later, John **3** … (*fight*) in another country and he **4** … (*forget*) about the worm. Meanwhile, the worm grew and grew. It **5** … (*eat*) cows, sheep and even children! Sir John **6** … (*come*) home to kill the beast and everyone **7** … (*be*) very happy and thanked Sir John for his bravery.

4 Read

Read the poem again and answer the questions.

1 Do you think the worm was real?
2 If it wasn't a worm, what could the animal have been?
3 What did the worm like to do?
4 What did the worm look like?
5 What sort of man was John Lambton?
6 What did Sir John do to the worm?

5 Use of English

Match the highlighted words in the poem with words of a similar meaning below. Use your dictionary to help you.

1 courageous   5 look around
2 strong   6 danger
3 frightening   7 sound
4 terrible

36

6 Pronunciation Stressed and unstressed words

Listen to the stressed and unstressed words in the lines of the poem.

He <u>caught</u> a <u>fish</u> upon his <u>hook</u>.
But <u>Lambton</u> had no <u>fear</u>.

7 🗨 **Talk**

Practise a verse of the poem with a partner.
Where are the stressed words?

Just what kind of fish it was
Young Lambton could not tell
He couldn't be bothered to carry it home
So he threw it down a well.

37 8 Listen

Now listen to this verse and check your answers.

9 Talk

Practise reading the poem out loud with your partner. Remember to stress the important words to add rhyme and rhythm to the verse.

10 🗨 **Values** Being courageous

Why was Sir John courageous?
How can we be courageous in life?

11 🗨 **Talk**

Talk about which pictures show courage and why.

6 Choose a project

1 My mythical creature

1 Look back at the mythical creatures you have learnt about in the unit. They often have a mix of human and animal characteristics.

2 Draw your mythical creature. Think about whether it is a monstrous animal or a kind animal.

3 Think of a name for your creature and write a physical description.

4 Write about its positive and negative traits. Is it friendly/unfriendly? patient/impatient?
Remember to use prefixes.

5 Display your picture and description on the classroom walls for your classmates to read, or publish it in the school magazine.

2 A short story: Practice makes perfect

1 Write a story about how practise makes perfect.

2 Think of a sport you play or a hobby you have. Explain why you like it.

3 Describe the difficulties this sport or hobby has. What was difficult for you when you started? **Remember** to use conjunctions to link your ideas.

4 Explain how you practise/or practised very hard to overcome the difficulties.

5 The ending line should be 'Practice makes perfect!'

Reflect on your learning

What lessons can we learn about life from myths and fables?

1 Look back at the unit and answer the question above.

2 Use prefixes to make these adjectives negative.

honest   kind   fair   agree   responsible   friendly

3 Write four sentences about your personality using the adjectives studied in the unit.

4 What do Cyclops, Medusa and a unicorn look like? Write a short description of each.

5 Complete these sentences with the correct conjunction.

a I knew my friend needed help ___ he called my name.

b I am a very impatient person ___ I can't wait for anything!

c Medusa was sent to the end of Earth ___ the blind monsters lived.

e The Cyclops gave away their eye ___ they could see the future.

6 Write sentences in the past continuous to explain what your family were doing when the phone rang last night.

> When the phone rang, I was doing my homework.

7 What lesson did the girl learn in the story *Feathers in the Wind*?

LOOk what I can do!

Write or show examples in your notebook.

1 I can talk about and describe mythical creatures.

2 I can understand fables from around the world and the lessons they teach us.

3 I can tell an anecdote about a personal experience.

4 I can write a short story.

5 I can understand simple proverbs.

6 I can understand a poem about a mythical creature.

Review 3

38 **1** **Listen**

Listen and number the pictures.

| explorer | artist | film director | scientist |

38 **2** Listen again. Draw a table like the one below and write the profession in each picture and its qualities.

	Profession	Qualities
1	...	brave and ...

3 **Use of English**

Choose the correct words.

1 A *must be/can't be* an explorer because he's very brave.

2 B *can't be/might be* a scientist because she's got paint on her clothes.

3 C *can't be/must be* a film director because he has a large camera.

4 D *might be/can't be* an artist because he's wearing a white coat.

4 **Vocabulary**

Read the clues and guess the word.

1 Someone who writes music.

2 A more interesting adjective than **pretty**.

3 Use a prefix to make the negative of **friendly**.

4 Use a prefix to make the negative of **honest**.

5 A person who looks after people has this quality.

6 A short story which has animals as the main characters and a moral to the story.

5 💬 Talk

In pairs, use question tags to check information.

> The explorer is very brave and determined, isn't he?

6 Use of English

Choose the correct word.

When I was about eight years old, I (1) *went / go* on a school trip to a Safari Park. (2) *When / Where* we (3) *arrived / was arriving* a guide showed us to the safari bus which we were going to tour the park on. (4) *Finally / First* we drove through the African reserve and saw the (5) *spectacular / nice* white rhino herd. We saw giraffes and zebras too. Then we noticed that a lioness (6) *walked / was walking* near the bus, (7) *so / if* the driver slowed down and we checked that the windows were closed. (8) *First / Then* the lioness just (9) *lay down / was lying down* in front of the bus, (10) *but / so* we had to stop and wait for her to move. We waited for 15 minutes and there was a line of cars behind us! You need to be very (11) *honest / patient* when you visit a Safari Park!

7 📝 Punctuation Direct speech

Write the sentences with the correct punctuation in your notebooks.

1 I'd love to be an explorer he said
2 I passed my piano exam she said happily
3 For your homework, please do some research about Medusa the teacher said
4 **A:** What do you think about Billy the football captain asked

   B: He's a great player and very reliable replied the manager
5 Quick said the captain drop the anchor

8 📝 Write

Write a short story about a day you visited a zoo, a farm or a safari park.

- Who did you go with?
- What did you see?
- Describe what you saw.
- Did anything unusual or funny happen?

9 💬 Talk

Look at Unit 6. Discuss in pairs which fable or myth you liked best.
Give reasons for your answer.

7 Ancient civilisations

We're going to:

talk and find out about ancient civilisations
read a text about The Egyptian Pyramids
give a presentation about life in ancient times

interview a partner about a discovery
write a newspaper report
understand and talk about an extract from a book.

1 Talk about it 💬 Do you recognise these buildings?

Where are they? Do you know which civilisations built them?

39 2 Listen

Listen to the information about these buildings.
Match the names with the pictures.

> The Colosseum   The Sphinx   The Pyramids   An aqueduct

39 3 📝 Match the sentences with a building from Activity 1.
Listen again and check your answers.

1 These were the stone tombs for the Pharaohs.
2 People believed that this creature guarded the tomb of the Pharaoh.
3 It's quite similar in shape to a modern football stadium.
4 They were built to provide a fresh water supply.
5 It was a place where people went for entertainment.

Use of English

Subordinate clauses think, know, believe

People **believed that** this creature guarded the Pharaoh's tomb.

4 Look at the *Use of English* box and match the sentence halves for you.

1 I think that   **a** the Sphinx guarded the tomb of the King.

2 I know that   **b** the Colosseum is similar in shape to a football stadium.

3 I believe that   **c** aqueducts transported fresh water to Roman cities.

5 💬 **Talk**

Are these facts **true** or **false**? Use subordinate clauses to talk about them.
Use the drawings in Activity 6 to help you.

Is it true that ...

... all the organs were taken out of the Pharaoh's body before mummification?

... the ancient Egyptians used pictures and not words to show ideas?

... zero is not used in Roman numerals?

... it took one month to make a mummy?

6 Word study Ancient objects and buildings

Match the definitions with the correct picture. Check your ideas from Activity 5.

1 This is where Romans liked to wash and bathe.

2 A slave who fought against wild animals in an amphitheatre.

3 These are the numbers used by Romans. It has seven digits and no zero.

4 The liver, stomach and lungs of a mummy, but not the heart were put in this.

5 This is Egyptian writing. They used pictures to show objects, ideas and sounds.

6 This is the body of a person that has been preserved. It took three months to do.

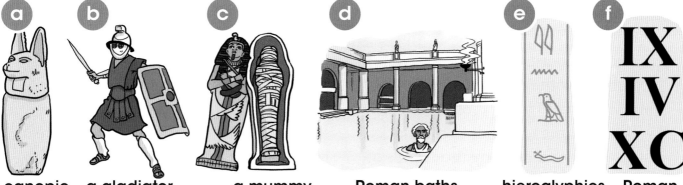

a a canopic jar   **b** a gladiator   **c** a mummy   **d** Roman baths   **e** hieroglyphics   **f** Roman numerals

2 Egyptian pyramids

1 Talk about it
  Use a **KWL** chart to discuss and write notes about:

(K) What you already **know** about The Pyramids.

(W) What you **want** to learn about The Pyramids.

(L) What you have **learned** about The Pyramids
(complete this when you have finished the lesson)

K	W	L

Reading strategy:
Use your own knowledge

Discuss what you already know
about a topic. Think of questions
you'd like to find the answer to in
the text.

2 Read

Read the text. Check your ideas
and try to find the answers to your
questions from Activity 1.

The Egyptian Pyramids were built as tombs for the pharaohs and their queens. The largest pyramid, The Great Pyramid of Giza, is on the west side of the River Nile and was built for the Pharaoh Khufu. It was over 140 metres high when it was first built and was made from over two million blocks of rock.

Archaeologists don't know exactly how they were built, but The Great Pyramid of Giza took a very long time to build! Large blocks of stone were moved by thousands of workers. In fact, archaeologists think it took about 20 000 workers twenty-three years to build this pyramid! When the pyramid was almost finished, a special block of gold was placed on top.

Inside the tomb, there were storage rooms for objects the king would need after he died. The tombs were filled with treasures as well as everyday objects. There were magnificent golden chariots, royal thrones, statues, weapons and jewellery. As well as clothing, perfumes, games, food and musical instruments. There were even mummified cats which were thought to protect the Pharaohs.

3 Read the text again. Answer these questions

1 Who were The Pyramids built for and why?

2 How long did it take to build The Great Pyramid of Giza?

3 What was special about the top of the pyramid?

4 What were the tombs filled with?

5 Why were cats mummified?

Use of English

Past simple passive

We use the **past simple passive** when the focus is on the past action and not *who* was doing the action.

The Great Pyramid of Giza **was built** on the west side of the River Nile.

When the person who did the action is important, we can add **by**.

Large blocks of stone **were moved** by thousands of workers.

4 Look at the *Use of English* box. How do you form the past simple passive? How many examples of the past simple passive can you find in the text?

5 Complete the information about how The Pyramids were built using the correct form of the passive.

First of all a perfect square (**1**) was marked (*mark*) in the desert sand. Then large blocks of stone (**2**) … (*move*) by thousands of workers to build the first layer. Next, ramps (**3**) … (*made*) to transport the stone to the next level of the pyramid. When the pyramid (**4**) … almost … (*finish*) a block of gold (**5**) … (*place*) on top.

6 Talk

What have you learned about The Pyramids? Talk with your partner and complete the *What I learned* section in your KWL chart.

③ Everyday life in ancient times

1 Talk about it 💬 Discuss everyday life in your town or city.

Talk about the subjects below.

> clothes   food   houses   jobs   pets   entertainment

2 📝 **Word study** Ancient Rome

Look at the picture of everyday life in ancient Rome. How is it different to your town? What words below can you find in the picture? If you are not sure about a word then listen to Ryan's presentation and explanation to help you.

> togas   tunics   bread   sandals   olives   meat   baths   chariot
> gladiator   farmer   soldier   merchant   engineer   villas

Listening strategy: Listen for clues

Listening for words that you already know can help you complete an activity.

40 3 Listen to Part 1 of Ryan's presentation about life in ancient Rome. Order the different parts of his presentation below. Listen carefully for clues (*food, a job*).

   a Typical food ___   **c** Roman houses _1_   **e** Clothes ___
   b Common jobs ___   **d** Entertainment ___

4 💬 **Talk**

Compare your everyday life to life in ancient Rome. Use **whereas**, **too**, **both**.

> Most days I wear jeans and a t-shirt, **whereas** the Romans wore tunics or togas.

41 5 Listen to Part 2 of Ryan's presentation. How does ancient Rome still influence modern-day culture? Complete the sentences.

   1 The Romans showed us how to build …
   2 They showed us how to transport water via …
   3 They showed us how to heat …
   4 We still play Roman games such as …
   5 Roman numerals are still used on …

6 💬 AB 1+2 **Word study** Roman numerals

Look at the Roman numerals. Write Roman numerals for your partner to work out.

   1 I   **3** III   **4** IV   **5** V   **6** VI   **7** VII   **8** VIII   **9** IX   **10** X
   15 XV   **50** L   **90** XC   **100** C   **500** D   **1000** M

Present it!

Life in your country in ancient times
- Choose a period of history in your country.
- Research the following: clothing, food, housing, jobs, pets and entertainment.
- Find or draw pictures to show the class.
- Compare life in the past with the present. Use time expressions.
- Talk for three minutes about your topic.

Speaking tip

Talking about a topic
When you give a factual presentation, talk about a variety of ideas on the topic to keep your audience interested.

1 Talk about it 💬 Have your ever discovered something interesting or of value, perhaps on a beach or in an old toy box?

2 Read

Read the report below about the discovery of Tutankhamun's tomb. Make a note of the treasures which were found inside.

King Tut's Tomb Discovered!

Yesterday, on the 24th November 1922, the archaeologist Howard Carter discovered the tomb of King Tutankhamun in the Valley of the Kings where many of the pharaohs were buried. The tomb was so small that it was not discovered for over 3000 years!

Tutankhamun became Pharaoh of Egypt when his father died in 1337 BCE. He was only nine years old! His death at the age of eighteen is still a mystery to scientists. Some believe he died from an infection in a broken leg others think he died from a blow to the head.

Howard Carter and his team were amazed by the treasures inside the tomb. 'It was like entering a time machine,' said Carter. 'We can now learn so much about daily life in Ancient Egypt.'

More than 3000 treasures were found in the tomb. On the walls there were hieroglyphics, a golden chariot, weapons, jewellery and a throne. There was even a board game to play called Senet – a popular game in Ancient Egypt. The most incredible discovery though was the mummy of Tutankhamun and the solid gold face mask.

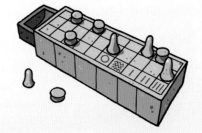

3 Read

Read the text and complete the facts below.

1 The tomb was discovered *on 24th November 1922*. (*When?*)
2 It was discovered ___ (*Who?*)
3 It was located ___ (*Where?*)
4 Many treasures were found in the tomb such as ___ (*What?*)

4

Read the text again and decide which of these sentences are fact (F), and which are opinion (O).

1 More than 3000 treasures were found in the tomb. F
2 Some believe he died from an infection.
3 Tutankhamun became King when his father died in 1337 BCE.
4 'It was like entering a time machine.'
5 Others think he died from a blow to the head.

5 📝 Write

Match the sentences below with the correct category.

1 Young boy finds gold Roman coins in his garden!
2 'It was the most beautiful thing I had ever seen!' said Ana.
3 Some people can't believe he found the treasure.
4 Yesterday morning, the treasure chest was found on the beach.

a fact
an opinion
a headline
a quotation

📝 **Write** A newspaper report about a discovery

- Invent or write about a real discovery.
- Make a list of the facts: What was discovered? When was it discovered? Where was it discovered? Who discovered it?
- Include facts and opinions.
- Include quotations from the person who made the discovery.
- Think of an interesting headline for the report.
- Don't forget to use past tenses.
- Draw pictures of the treasure and display the reports in your classroom.

Writing tip

Use the past simple and past simple passive when you are telling a story.

The tomb **was discovered** in 1922. The most incredible discovery **was** the mummy of Tutankhamun.

1 Talk about it   What famous discoveries have been made in your country?

What was discovered? Who discovered it?

42   2   Read and listen

Read and listen to the text. Then answer the questions after each part.

Vocabulary

fade: lose brightness

musty: an unpleasant wet smell

inspect: look at

cobweb:

There's a Pharaoh in Our Bath!

1   The lid of the cobwebbed coffin was slowly pushed back and the two men laid it carefully on the museum floor. They stared inside at the beautifully painted Ancient Egyptian mummy-case, covered with picture-writing.

Daylight was already beginning to fade from the musty storeroom. The other museum staff had gone home and the only company left with the two men now were the stacks of old mummy-cases, ancient skeletons and a large, stuffed rhinoceros.

Professor Jelly pulled the lamp closer and inspected the hieroglyphs. The light shimmered across his moon-like face.

'What does it say?' demanded Grimstone. The head of the museum's Ancient Egyptian collection stared over Jelly's shoulder. 'Is it the mummy of the missing Pharaoh?'

1 What objects are in the storeroom?
2 How is the mummy-case described?
3 What are they looking for?

2 Professor Jelly took a sweet from his jacket-pocket, popped it in his mouth and bent over the mummy-case. 'Hmmmm, hazelnut crunch. Now, this squiggly bit here says *May perfumed flowers be crushed beneath his feet.* Very poetic.'

'But who's inside?' Grimstone barked impatiently, and his great winged eyebrows crashed together over his hooded eyes and hawk-nose. He stabbed a thin finger at one side of the coffin. 'What about here? What does it say? It looks important.'

Professor Jelly sucked noisily on his sweet. 'That bit there?'

'Yes!'

'That says *Please keep this way up at all times.*'

'What!' yelled Grimstone.

'And that bit,' continued the professor, waving at some faded hieroglyphs with a pudgy hand, 'that bit there says *Not to be opened before Christmas.*'

For a few seconds Grimstone was stunned then his eyes glinted dangerously. 'You're making this up, Jelly, aren't you?'

The professor straightened his tubby frame. 'Of course I'm making it up. Stop pestering me and let me study it properly. This mummy has been stuck here for seventy years already, ever since it was first brought to the museum from Ancient Egypt for the collection. A few more minutes' wait won't hurt.'

4 Who is getting impatient?
5 Which of the hieroglyphic messages does Professor Jelly invent?

> **Vocabulary**
>
> **squiggly:** lines curving up and down
> **glint:** look bright

105

3 'This could be the discovery of the century. It could make our fortunes. We could be millionaires. The clue to a fabulous treasure is in that coffin,' he turned his back to the professor. 'Come on Jelly, get a move on.'

The professor was still translating the hieroglyphs on the coffin's side. '*He who opens this coffin will be cursed by Anubis.* There now, just our luck. We're going to be cursed by Anubis.'

'Who's Anubis?' demanded Grimstone.

'He was the Ancient Egyptian God of the Dead – had a head like a jackal.'

Jeremy Strong

> **Vocabulary**
>
> **jackal:** a wild dog
>
> **devour:** to eat something quickly

6 What does Grimstone think they could find in the coffin?

7 Who was Anubis?

3 💬 **Talk**

What do you think happened when Professor Jelly finally opened the coffin?

4 **Word study** Adjectives

Match the adjectives with the correct part of the body or face. Use your dictionary and the illustrations to help you. Then check your answers with the text.

1	moon-like	**a**	eyes
2	winged	**b**	finger
3	hooded	**c**	face
4	hawk	**d**	eyebrows
5	tubby	**e**	frame
6	pudgy	**f**	nose

43 5 Pronunciation Identifying tone

Listen to the direct speech from the story and match with an emotion.

> angry   excited   worried   impatient

1 'But who's inside?'
2 'Of course I'm making it up.'
3 'This could be the discovery of the century. It could make our fortunes.'
4 'You're making this up, Jelly, aren't you?'

6 Write

Use subordinate clauses to complete the sentences about your opinion of the story. Make negative sentences too

> think   hope   believe   know

1 I *think that* the professor will find something in the coffin.
2 I … Grimstone is very impatient.
3 I … the mummy has been in the storeroom for seventy years.
4 I … Professor Jelly can translate hieroglyphs.
5 I … that the hieroglyph message wasn't *Not to be opened before Christmas.*

7 Write a paragraph about what you think happens when the Professor opens the coffin.

> It took a while for Professor Jelly to open the coffin, but when he did …

8 Values The importance of being patient

In the story, Grimstone is very impatient. Read and choose **a** or **b** to find out how patient you are.

1 **a** I hate waiting for people.
  b I don't mind waiting for people.

2 **a** I don't like long journeys.
  b I enjoy long journeys.

3 **a** I like to do my homework quickly.
  b I take my time doing my homework.

4 **a** If I want something new, I want it immediately.
  b I don't mind waiting until my birthday to receive new things.

> **Key:**
> If your answers are mainly **a**, then you are very impatient. How do you think you could be more patient?
> If they are mainly **b** then you are a very patient person.

6 Choose a project

1 A famous building or statue

1 Find out about an ancient building or statue in your town or city.

2 Research it in your local library or on the Internet. Find out the following information:

When was it built? Who was it built by? What was it built for?
If it is a building, is it still used today?

3 If possible, visit the building or statue. Draw a picture of it or take a photo.

4 What is your opinion of this building or statue?

5 Present your work to your class and then display your work in your classroom.

2 Egyptian hieroglyphics: Break the code!

These are the symbols used in Egyptian writing.

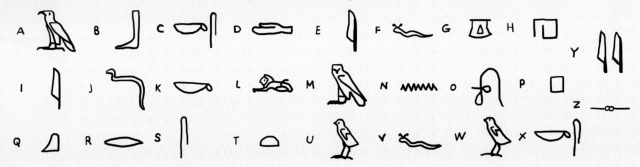

1 Can you read these coded words?

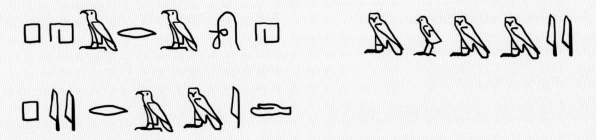

2 Write your own codes for your classmates to guess. You could write your name, your favourite food, sport or singer in hieroglyphics.

Reflect on your learning

What can we see of ancient civilisations in our culture today?

1 Write a definition for the following words:

pyramid   Roman numerals   hieroglyphics   pharaoh

2 Write four sentences describing how the pyramids were built using the following verbs in the past simple passive.

build   move   made   finish   place

3 Answer these questions: **What did people wear in ancient Rome? What did they eat? What were common jobs and professions?**

4 Write the following numbers in Roman numerals:

17   23   14   115   1550

5 Write four facts about the discovery of Tutankhamen's tomb.

6 Which part of the face do these adjectives and expressions describe?

winged   hooded   hawk   moon-like

L👀k what I can do!

Write or show examples in your notebook.

1 I can understand and talk about ancient civilisations.
2 I can read and understand a text about The Egyptian Pyramids.
3 I can give a presentation about life in my country in ancient times.
4 I can interview my partner about a discovery.
5 I can write a newspaper report.
6 I can understand and talk about an extract from a book.

8 Weather and climate

We're going to:

talk about the weather and temperatures around the world

listen and present a newscast about extreme weather

read a text about rainforests

read and learn about rainforest animals

research and write a description of a rainforest animal

understand and talk about a poem.

1 Talk about it Have you ever experienced extreme weather conditions?

How did you protect yourself?

2 Word study Extreme weather

Match the words with the pictures.

> flood   tornado   blizzard   drought   typhoon   sandstorm

a

b

c

d

e

f

44 3 Listen

Listen and match each speaker with the weather.

4 Read the weather fact box below. Can you remember which facts are **true** or **false**? Listen again and check your answers.

Fact or fiction?

1 A sandstorm can travel at about 80 kilometres per hour.
2 Blizzards are tropical storms.
3 There could be power cuts during a blizzard.
4 Other names for a typhoon are: hurricane and cyclone.
5 During a typhoon there are high winds and heavy rain.
6 Monsoon season is when there is no rain.

5 **Word study** Weather collocations

Check the words below in your dictionary and complete the sentences. More than one adjective might be possible for some sentences.

> heavy high severe torrential strong violent

1 A blizzard is a ___ snowstorm.
2 ___ rain and ___ winds are experienced during a hurricane.
3 When a river overflows ___ flooding can take place.
4 ___ rain can cause flooding.
5 A typhoon is a ___ storm.

6 **Listen**

Listen to Habib talk about the things you should/shouldn't do when there is a sandstorm. Write the actions in the correct column in your notebook.

> stay indoors drive your car keep warm wear a mask
> use your camel to protect you put a coat on
> protect your body shut the windows

Should ...	Should not ...

7 **Talk**

Use weather collocations to describe the type of weather you experience in your country. What should/shouldn't you do in extreme weather conditions?

2 Rainforests

1 Talk about it 💬 What do you know about rainforests?

Talk about where they are and why they are special. What problems are there?

2 Read

Read the text and check your answers to Activity 1.

A Rainforests are very large, wet forests found close to the equator in South East Asia, West Africa and Central and South America. They have very high temperatures and it rains all year round. In a year it can rain as much as 260 centimetres!

B The rainforest is divided up into three layers. The canopy is the top layer of the trees where most of the animals live. These trees can be more than 30 metres high and it is the noisiest layer of the rainforest. The understory is underneath the canopy and has some shorter trees and bushes and the third layer is the forest floor. It has very little sunlight and is the quietest layer of the rainforest.

C There are as many as 30 million types of plants and animals which live in the tropical rainforests. The tiny red-eyed tree frog in the photo is just one of the spectacular amphibians that live there.

D Rainforests help to protect the world's **climate** because they take **carbon dioxide**, a **greenhouse gas** from the air, and release oxygen for us to breathe. Many of the **natural resources** we need such as vital medicines and food come from the rainforests too.

E Unfortunately, these rainforests are disappearing. Every second an area the size of a football field is either cut down for wood to make furniture, to build houses or to be cleared for farming animals. Action needs to be taken to **protect** the rainforests, now!

3 💬 **Talk**

What is happening to the rainforest? What do you think about it, and why?

Reading strategy: Giving your opinion

Evaluate texts, make notes and say what you think about them.

4 Match the questions with the correct paragraph from the text.

1 Why are rainforests important to us?

2 What are the layers of the rainforest?

3 What is a rainforest?

4 What is happening to the rainforests?

5 What lives in the rainforests?

5 **Word study** The environment

Match the words in blue in the text with the definitions below.

1 a gas which we breathe out

2 weather conditions in a particular area

3 a gas which keeps heat in Earth's atmosphere

4 to defend something

5 things such as water, forests and minerals which are in a place and can be used by people

6 📝 💬 **Values** Looking after our world

• Think about and discuss what you can do to help protect the rainforests.

• Write a list of things we can do.

• Display your ideas with your drawings of the rainforests and animals which live in them. Use these pictures to give you ideas.

3 Extreme weather

1 Talk about it 💬 Is the weather different for each season in your country?

How good are weather reports – does the presenter always get it right?!

2 Listen

Listen to the weather reports and match them with the correct country.

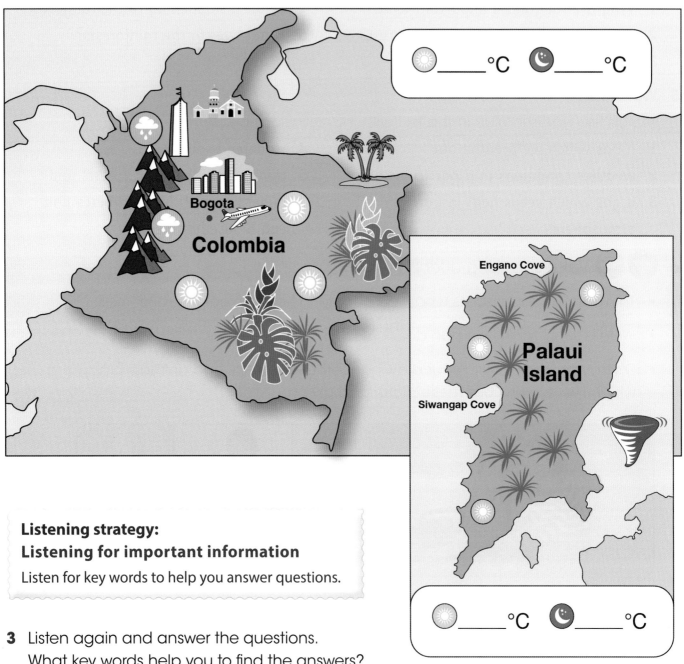

Listening strategy:
Listening for important information

Listen for key words to help you answer questions.

3 Listen again and answer the questions.
What key words help you to find the answers?

1 What is the temperature in the day and at night in the two countries?

2 What advice does the man give for people living in Colombia?

3 What should people do on Palaui Island?

46 4 📝 Use of English

Look at the *Use of English* box and use the adverbs of degree to complete these sentences. Then listen again and check.

1 Tomorrow will be ___ warm.
2 It might be ___ wet.
3 In the evening it will be ___ cold.
4 Tomorrow there will be ___ heavy rain and high winds.
5 It will be ___ humid.

5 💬 Talk

Discuss what you like most and what you like least about the climate in your country. Give reasons for your answers using adverbs of degree.

> ## Use of English
>
> **Adverbs of degree**
>
> **quite   a little   very   extremely**
>
> Adverbs give more information about adjectives or verbs. Adverbs of degree tell us the strength of something that happens.

47 6 📝 Pronunciation Stressing important information

Listen and pick out the stressed words. Then practise with your partner.

1 We start with a *warning* about a typhoon which is coming in across the south of the island.
2 The typhoon will be the worst at 4 pm.
3 So, please stay indoors during the storm.
4 The temperature will drop to about 23° C at night.

> ## Speaking tip
>
> Rehearse your newscast a number of times before the presentation. 'Practice makes perfect!'

Present it!

Choose A or B:

A Write a weather report for a country you know:
- Choose a country and draw a map. Decide what the weather will be like.
- Talk about what the weather will be like and the temperature.
- Rehearse your newscast. Practise stressing the important words.

B Research an extreme weather event:
- Find out on the Internet or in your local library how extreme weather events happen and their effects.
- Find pictures of this type of weather.
- Include advice on what people should do.
- Rehearse your newscast. Practise stressing the important words.

115

4 Rainforest animals

1 Talk about it 💬 What kind of animals live in rainforests?

Which part of the forest do you think they live in – the canopy or on the forest floor?

2 📝 Read

Read Mina's description of the spider monkey.
What adjectives does she use to describe it?

1 _Location_

Spider monkeys live in the tropical rainforests of Central and South America. They usually live high up in cecropia trees and almost never come to the ground. Some are endangered because their habitat is being destroyed.

2 _____

They have got thick, black, brown or red fur and four long limbs. They've also got a very strong, long tail which they use to hang upside down from the branches of the trees.

3 _____

Their favourite food is fruit which they pick with their long arms, but they also eat seeds, nuts, plants and honey.

4 _____

Spider monkeys live in groups of 20 or more and are **diurnal** (active during the day). They love swinging from tree to tree!

5 _____

However, these monkeys are not very sociable. When they see a human, they often scream or jump up and down shaking the branches of the trees!

3 📝 Choose a heading for each of the sections 1 to 5 in the text.

a Diet **b** Appearance **c** Location **d** Behaviour **e** Curious fact

Unit 8 Lesson 4 Use of English: adjective order Read: The spider monkey Write: a description

Adjective order When we use more than one adjective to describe a noun the adjectives need to be in the following order:

1		2		3		4		5		6		7		8		9
Number	→	Opinion	→	Size	→	Age	→	Shape	→	Colour	→	Origin	→	Material	→	Noun
Three		*fabulous*		*big*		*old*		*fat*		*brown*		*Costa Rican*		*furry*		*sloths*

4 **Read**

Read the *Fact file* about sloths. Match the adjectives in red to the numbers in the *Use of English* box.

Fact file

Sloths

- The two-toed and three-toed sloths live in the rainforest of Costa Rica.
- They have got a **thick**, **grey**, **furry coat** and **long**, **sharp claws** and very **tiny ears**, so they don't hear very well. They have got a **short**, **flat head** but have got excellent eyesight and a good sense of smell.
- Sloths are herbivores but they don't eat a lot. They eat leaves, fruit and other plants very slowly with their **small teeth**.
- They spend most of their time hanging upside down in the trees sleeping! Even when they are awake they don't move!
- A sloth can sleep for 15 to 18 hours each day! They are also the slowest mammals on Earth. It takes them a month to move 1 kilometre!

Writing tip

Use lots of adjectives to make your description more interesting. Use commas between them when needed.

Write a description of a rainforest animal

- Choose a rainforest animal.
- Find out if the animal is an endangered species.
- Find out about it on the Internet or in a library.
- Organise your writing into paragraphs. Check your adjective order.
- Draw a picture of the animal.
- Display your description and picture in your class.

5 Poems: *A Visit with Mr Tree Frog* and *If I Were a Sloth*

1 Talk about it What's your favourite animal? Is a sloth a mammal?

Which group of animals do frogs belong to? Think of more examples for each.

> reptiles   mammals   amphibians   fish

48 **2 Read and listen**

Read and listen to the poem. Match the illustrations with a line in the poem.

A Visit with Mr Tree Frog

I have a tiny buddy,
2 Tree Frog is his name.
He flew in from Brazil
4 In his tiny toy plane.

He rattles when he speaks.
6 He's greener than green grass.
He is a tree hugger
8 That really is first class.

He has **bright** orange toes
10 That **wiggle** in the night.
He's a mellow fellow
12 That does not like to fight.

He dines on crickets and flies,
14 And moths are for a treat.
He's not the average guy
16 You find on city streets.

Vocabulary

buddy: friend
mellow: smooth and soft
guy: man

He was born in a forest,
18 A forest with **warm** rain.
He is an earthly treasure
20 That has a claim to fame.

He has a magic slime
22 That can **cure** laziness.
His slime can cure the world,
24 And yet he's poisonous.

His eyes are really red.
26 They pop up like snaps.
He **blinks** when he's resting.
28 During the day he naps.

He is here to brainstorm
30 About our planet so green.
He's a **wonder** of our world.
32 The cutest I've ever seen.

Kathy Paysen

48 3 Pronunciation

Listen again and find words in the poem that rhyme with the words below.

| class | streets | fame | fight |
| plane | poisonous | seen | naps |

> ### Vocabulary
> **slime:** a sticky liquid
> **snaps:** photos taken with a polaroid camera that pop up

4 Word study

Match the words in blue in the poem with the definitions below.

1 intense (colour)
2 open and close your eyes quickly
3 a nice temperature
4 to heal something
5 to move quickly from side to side
6 a surprising thing

5 Talk

What is the poet's opinion of the tree frog? What do you think of the tree frog?

119

Read and listen to the poem. Put the illustrations in order.

a

If I Were a Sloth

1 If I were a sloth
Hanging from a tree,
I could show the world
My personality.

5 I would see the world
Hanging upside down,
Dangling like a coconut,
High above the ground.

9 I would nap all day
In the canopy,
Of the Rain Forest
Cecropia trees.

13 I would move real slow,
Slow as slow can be,
Hiding from jaguar,
My fierce enemy.

17 I am nocturnal.
I only play at night.
When the sun goes down,
I like to grab a bite.

Kathy Paysen

21 I can whistle like a bird.
I am really rare.
With my long, long arms,
People like to stare.

25 In my grey-green coat,
I will always thrive.
I'm a little sloth.
I make the jungle jive.

b

c

d

e

Unit 8 Lesson 5 Poem: *If I Were a Sloth* **Vocabulary:** action verbs and similes

7 📝 **Word study** Action verbs

Use these action verbs from the poem in the correct form to complete the sentences. Use your dictionary to check for meaning.

> hang   move   play   whistle   stare

1 Hedgehogs ___ very slowly.
2 Why is that girl ___ at me? Do I look funny?
3 Monkeys use their arms to ___ from tree branches.
4 Children like to ___ hide and seek.
5 My parrot ___ at me when I come into the room!

8 Read

Read the poems again and compare the tree frog and the sloth. Are the sentences **true** or **false**?

1 They both live in the rainforest.
2 They are both poisonous.
3 They are both nocturnal.
4 They both make strange noises.

9 📝 **Word study** Similes

We compare two things by using the word **like**. Look at the examples from the poems. Complete the similes below using your own words.

> They pop up **like** snaps.   Dangling **like** a coconut.

1 The sloth is furry like ___ .
2 The sloth is lazy like ___ .
3 The frog is green like ___ .
4 The frog's slime is magic like ___ .

10 📝 **Write**

Write more similes about the sloth and the tree frog.

11 💬 **Talk**

Which rainforest animal do you like best. Give reasons for your answers.

6 Choose a project

1 Chart weather conditions

1 Make a chart like this one to display in your classroom. You need to write the number of days for the month you have decided to study the weather conditions in your town or city, and symbols for the weather you usually experience at this time of year.

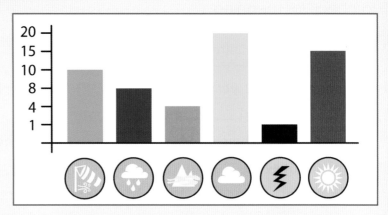

2 Take turns with your classmates to chart the weather each day with small coloured pieces of card.

3 The volunteer should tell the class about the weather conditions each day.

> Today, it's hot, humid and overcast.

4 At the end of the month, write a report on the weather conditions you have experienced.

2 Raise money to help protect the rainforests

1 As you have learned in this unit, the rainforests are in great danger. These children have raised money to help protect the rainforest. Can you name each activity?

2 Discuss more ways in which you could raise money.

3 Vote on which fundraising activity you like best.

4 Organise your activity with the help of your teacher. You can then donate the money you raise to conservation groups which are working to protect the rainforests.

Reflect on your learning

How can we protect our planet?

1 Write four sentences about the seasonal weather in your country.

> In the summer, it's ...

2 Now add these adverbs of degree in your sentences.

quite   a little   very   extremely

3 Write four weather collocations.

4 What is happening to the rainforests? Give reasons why?

5 Write three examples of how you look after your world or three things you are going to do now you have finished the unit.

6 Complete these facts about a rainforest animal of your choice.

Name   Location   Appearance

Diet   Behaviour   Curious fact

7 Put these adjectives in order before the final noun.

small/two/furry toes

sharp/four/long claws

hairy/long/two/black arms

L👀k what I can do!

Write or show examples in your notebook.

> **1** I can talk about weather and temperatures.
> **2** I can present a newscast about extreme weather conditions.
> **3** I can read and give my opinion on the subject of the text.
> **4** I can understand a text about rainforest animals and discuss their behaviour.
> **5** I can research and write about a rainforest animal.
> **6** I can read and talk about a poem.

Review 4

50 **1** **Listen**

Listen and match the words with the pictures. Which are Egyptian and which are Roman?

chariot   hieroglyphics   tunic and toga   aqueduct   sphinx   canopic jar

50 **2** Listen again and decide if the sentences are **true** or **false**.

1 An aqueduct transported fresh water into the cities.

2 The chariot races were held in amphitheatres.

3 The tunic was longer than the toga.

4 The Pharaoh's organs were kept in the canopic jar.

5 Archaeologists know that the sphinx were built to guard the tombs.

3 **Talk**

In pairs, talk about what you can remember about everyday life in Rome.

I know that Romans wore tunics.   I think that ...   I believe that ...

4 Vocabulary

Read the clues and guess the word.

1 This word describes what happens after heavy rain.

2 The name for the Roman numeric system.

3 Another name for a snowstorm.

4 A type of weather which collocates with **high**.

5 A greenhouse gas.

6 A rainforest animal.

7 The top layer of the rainforest.

8 Two adjectives you can use to describe *claws*.

5 Use of English

Read and choose the correct word.

On my first trip to the rainforest, I (1) *was told / was telling* to cover my body at all times, but I got (2) *a little / very* hot and uncomfortable. I recommend that you wear a t-shirt during the day and cover up at night. However, you (3) *shouldn't / should* wear rubber boots or trekking boots all the time as the mosquitoes are (4) *a bit / extremely* hungry in the Amazon! You also need to check inside your boots when you wake up in the morning as (5) *tiny / huge* amphibians which are sometimes (6) *bite / poisonous* hide inside them. I (7) *was advised / told* by the guide to keep my rucksack closed at all times (8) *both / too* as all kinds of spiders and snakes can creep inside, so I did! Don't forget your raincoat either as it can rain (9) *a little / quite* heavily at times. You also need a good pair of sunglasses and a sunhat if you are on the river. You (10) *should / shouldn't* always drink water from a plastic bottle. Don't drink water from the tap in the hotel and never drink it from the river!

6 🗨 Talk

Read the text in Activity 5 again and talk about what you should/shouldn't do in the rainforest.

7 Use of English

Order these words correctly.

1 pink / frog / tiny / A / poisonous
2 has / long/ claws / sharp / It / got
3 sloths / Three / furry / brown
4 thick / Spider monkeys / have / brown / fur / got

8 📝 Write

Write a paragraph giving advice to people who are going to visit one of the places below. Use **should** and **shouldn't**.

- the beach
- the mountains
- the Arctic
- the desert

9 Planet Earth

We're going to:

talk about animal habitats
learn about food chains
read a text about animal camouflage

talk about caring for a pet
write a leaflet about a children's farm
read a poem about pets

1 Talk about it 💬 Do you live near any of the habitats below?

What is it like (hot/cold/dry)?

2 Word study Animal habitats

Match the animals with their habitat.

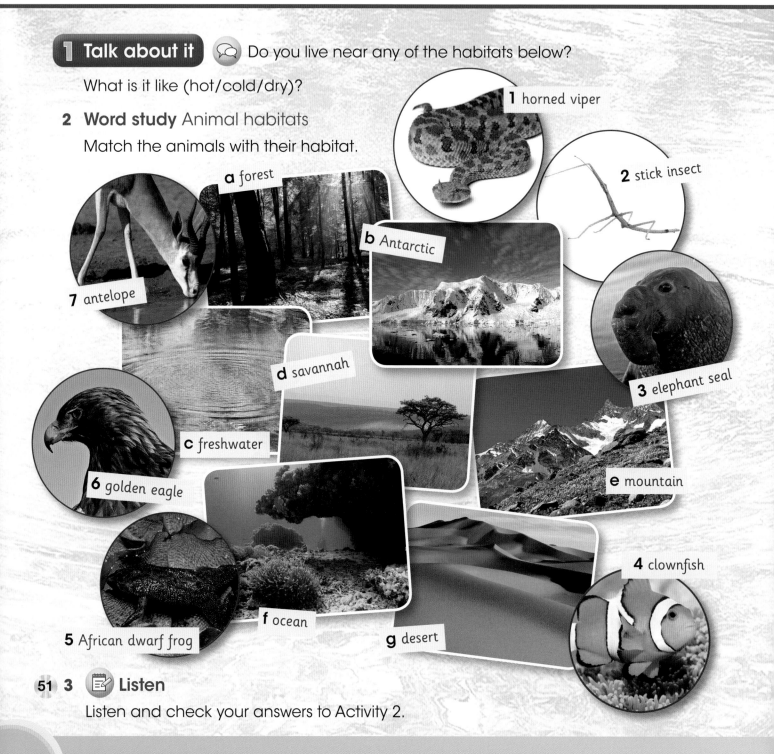

1 horned viper
2 stick insect
a forest
b Antarctic
7 antelope
3 elephant seal
d savannah
c freshwater
e mountain
6 golden eagle
4 clownfish
5 African dwarf frog
f ocean
g desert

51 **3** 📝 **Listen**

Listen and check your answers to Activity 2.

51 4 📝 Listen again and take notes. Can you add more animals to the different habitats?

	Type of animal	Name of animal	Habitat	Eats
1	amphibian			blood worms/water fleas
2		clownfish		algae

5 💬 Talk

Look at the food chain below. Can you explain it?

Reading strategy: Interpreting diagrams

Use reading texts to help you understand diagrams and flowcharts.

6 Read

Now read the text and check your answers to Activity 5.

A food chain shows us how living things get their food – who eats who! A food chain always starts with a plant which is called a **producer** because it makes its own food from the energy it gets from the sun. Consumers are the next link and there are usually three levels. The first group are **primary consumers**; herbivores such as a rabbit or a mouse which only eat plants. The second group are

secondary consumers which are carnivores. They eat the primary consumers. A **tertiary consumer** is usually a larger animal which eats the smaller animal. There are also consumers called omnivores which eat plants and meat and they can be secondary or tertiary consumers. Can you think of an example of one? Yes, humans of course!

7 📝 Order the food chains.

1   3

2

8 📝 🧪 Choose one of the habitats from Activity 2 and draw a diagram of a food chain. Label each part with the words in blue from the text.

9 💬 **Talking game**

What is it? Take turns to guess the animal. Your partner can ask *yes/no* questions.

> Does it live in the desert?
> Is it a mammal? Does it eat …?

Discuss what you can see.

2 **Read**

How do animals adapt to their environment? How do animals protect themselves?

Animal hide and seek!

Most animals need to be very clever in order to survive in the animal kingdom. One of their most amazing skills is called camouflage – their bodies copy the colour of their environment to hide from their predators or to help them hunt for their prey.

The chameleon can change its colour to copy all kinds of backgrounds. These colours protect it from predators.

The flower spider with its venomous fangs is expert at camouflage – it changes its colour to match the flower it is sitting on!

The cuttlefish with its green blood and three hearts is also excellent at camouflage. It can change colour in seconds but it can also change its body shape to look like something else when a hungry predator comes along! If a predator is chasing it, (it's a very fast swimmer) it shoots ink into the sea. This makes the water cloudy, so it can escape more easily.

3 Read the text again and find the following:

   1 Two things animals need to do in order to survive.

   2 Where the spider keeps its venom.

   3 Two strange characteristics of the cuttlefish.

   4 Another way in which the cuttlefish can camouflage itself.

4 [AB] Look at the *Use of English* box and match it with the animal it describes in the text. Find more examples in the text.

5 **Word study** Animal characteristics

Look at the animals below and use the words in the box to describe how these characteristics help them. Use **it/its** when you can.

> a furry coat   a long tail   big
> ears   stripes   scales   a hump

Use of English

it/its

We use **it** instead of the name of the person, place, object or animal, so that we don't repeat the name. We use **its** if something belongs to the person or animal.

It shoots ink into the sea.

The chameleon can change **its** colour to copy …

> A snake has got scales. It uses its scales to help it move and to keep cool.

6 Over to you

Find out how other animals have adapted to their environments.
Research one of the animals above or choose your own.
Present your findings to the class.

> Why has a zebra got stripes?   Why has a giraffe got a long neck?

1 Talk about it Have you got a pet or would you like to have a pet?

Make a list of the animals that make good pets.
Give reasons for your answers.

52 2 Listen

What is the listening text about? Match the children with their pets.

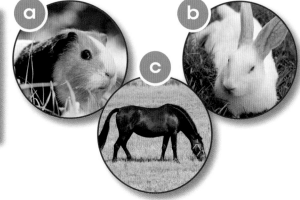

David   Hannah   Tilly

52 3 Word study Caring for pets

Match the correct word with each picture. Listen again and check your answers.

> feed   groom   clean   exercise   visit (the vet)   look after (teeth)

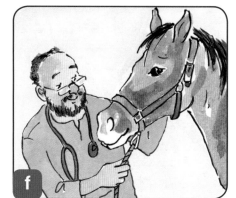

AB **must/should/ have to/need to**

To talk about obligation and necessity we can use **must**, **should** (modal verbs) and other verbs such as, **have (to)** and **need (to)**.

You **must** give your horse food every day.   You **have to** give your horse fresh water every day.

You **should** clean it when it is dirty.   You **need to** look after their teeth.

Remember to add **to** after **need** and **have**.

4   Look at the *Use of English* box and put the words below in order.

Advice for hamster owners

1   feed / your hamster / You / must / every day

2   put clean water / of his cage / at the side / need to / You

3   clean out / You / once a week / his cage / should

4   don't / You / – he will clean himself / groom the hamster / need to

5   You / so he gets exercise / should put / for him to play with / something in his cage

Present it!

How to look after a pet

• Either talk about your own pet, or choose a pet you would like.

• Brainstorm the types of care and attention this pet needs.

My pet's needs

feeding twice a day

• Prepare notes about caring for your pet using verbs to talk about obligation and necessity.

• You can use expressions to give advice too.

• Draw a picture to show how you care for your pet.

• Give your presentation in front of the class.

Speaking tip

Giving advice

It's best to use a brush or a special comb.

It's a good idea to check your horse's teeth.

It's important that a horse goes for regular check-ups at the vets.

1 Talk about it Have you ever visited a farm, zoo or safari park?

Was it a school or a family trip? What animals did you see? What did you do?

2 Read this leaflet about the opening of a wildlife park. Would you like to go there? What activities or animals attract your attention in the leaflet? Why?

DURDLE MOOR WILDLIFE PARK

Come and feed the goats and lambs!

Don't miss the tractor and trailer ride!

Be the first to collect the fresh eggs! Stroke the baby chicks!

There's lots to see at **Durdle Moor Wildlife Park**.

Come and see our llamas, racoons, meerkats and Egyptian fruit bats!

Ride our shire horse and don't leave without seeing our boa constrictor and Burmese python, or our birds of prey!

Opening Times

Sun–Sat 10 am – 6 pm

Closed Mondays (except bank holidays during school term time)

Prices:

Adults: £8   Pensioners: £6.50

Children (2 to 14yrs): £6

Under 2yrs: FREE ADMISSION

3 Read

Read the leaflet and answer **true** or **false**.

1 You can't touch the animals.

2 The farm is closed on Mondays.

3 There aren't any reptiles.

4 You can feed the lambs.

5 You have to pay for children under the age of two.

4 [1+2] Problem solving

1 A family of six want to spend the day at Durdle Moor farm. There are three adults, one is a pensioner and three children aged 1, 10 and 8. They have £40. How much money do they have left to spend at the farm once they have paid for their tickets?

2 Two elderly grandparents want to take their four grandchildren on an outing to the farm, but they're not sure if they have enough money. Their grandchildren are aged 2, 4, 8 and 15. Work out how much it will cost. Their budget is £40.

5 [AB] Write

Slogans are interesting sentences which attract people's attention. Look at the slogan below. Can you find more examples in the advertisement?

> **Come** and **feed** the goats and lambs!

> ### Writing tip
>
> Use imperative sentences to write your slogans.
>
> Come and ... !   Don't miss ... !
>
> Be the first ... !   Don't leave ... !

[✎] Write Design and write a leaflet

- Design and write a leaflet to advertise a local animal farm, animal sanctuary or safari park in your area.
- Make a list of special activities for children: feeding the animals, horse rides, etc.
- Write slogans to attract people's interest.
- Find photos from magazines of mammals, insects, birds and amphibians or draw your own pictures.
- Include information on opening times and prices.

1 Talk about it Have you ever asked for a pet that you couldn't have?

How did you feel? Why couldn't you have it?

53 **2 Read and listen**

Read and listen to the poem. Find the animals from the poems in the pictures.

Mum Won't Let Me Keep a Rabbit

Mum won't let me keep a rabbit,
She won't let me keep a bat,
She won't let me keep a porcupine
Or a water-rat.

I can't keep pigeons
And I can't keep snails,
I can't keep kangaroos
Or wallabies with nails.

She won't let me keep a rattlesnake
Or a viper in the house,
She won't let me keep a mamba
Or its meal, a mouse.

She won't let me keep a wombat
And it isn't very clear,
Why I can't keep iguanas,
Jellyfish or deer.

I can't keep a cockroach
Or a bumblebee,
I can't keep an earwig
A maggot or a flea.

I can't keep a wildebeest
And it's just my luck
I can't keep a mallard,
A dabchick or a duck.

She won't let me keep piranhas,
Toads or even frogs,
She won't let me keep an octopus
Or muddy water-hogs.

So out in the garden I keep a pet ant
And up in the attic A SECRET ELEPHANT!

Brian Patten

3 What animal does the poet keep in the attic? Reorder the letters to find out.

4 Pronunciation

Find words in the poem which rhyme with these animals.
Then listen and check.

1 bat **2** snails **3** deer **4** bumblebee **5** duck **6** water-hogs

5 📝 Put the animals from the poem into groups. Use your dictionary to
check the meaning of the words you don't know.

Mammals	Insects	Birds	Amphibians	Reptiles
	flea			

6 📝 **Write**

Write three sentences about the animals you'd like to keep from the poem,
and three about those you wouldn't like to keep.

> **I**'d like to keep a …   **I** wouldn't like to keep a …

7 Write a verse about the animals you are sure you can't keep in your house.
Try to make the words in line two and line four rhyme.

I can't keep a …
And I can't … *(rhyming word)*
I can't keep a …
Or a … with … *(rhyming word)*

8 📝 **Over to you**

Find out information about one of the
animals you haven't heard of before in
the poem. Write a paragraph about
it and find a picture.

Type of animal: Rabbit
Diet: grass, herbs, flowers
Habitat: fields
Behaviour: sleeps most of the day
Characteristics: small, brown, white
   or black fur, long ears, big feet,
   good sense of smell

Unit 9 Lesson 5 Poem: *Mum Won't Let Me Keep a Rabbit* **Pronunciation:** rhyming words **Read/Listen:** alliteration **Values:** taking care of animals
Write: animal verse

9 Read and listen

Read and listen to these examples of animal alliteration. Match with the correct illustration. What do you notice about the words?

1 Larry the lucky lion laughed loudly as he leaped over Lucy the lazy lizard while she lovingly licked a lemon lollipop.

2 Charlie the cheerful cheetah chose to chew cheese and cherries as he chomped his chops.

a

b

10 Choose the correct definition for alliteration.

a The words all rhyme.

b The main words all start with the same sound.

11 Look at the guide below then copy and complete the table.
You don't have to think of a word for every column.

Name	Size/shape	Colour	Animal	Action verb	Adverb/noun
Sid	(the) small	silver		slithers	slowly
Pete	(the) plump	purple		paints pictures	perfectly

12 Write your own animal alliteration. Use the guide to help you. Draw a picture to illustrate your alliteration.

13 **Values** Taking care of animals

Discuss the questions in groups.

1 Think about the horse that Tilly rescued in Lesson 3. How was she kind?

2 Why is it important to look after animals and pets?

3 What can having a pet at home teach you?

4 Is it good to keep pets? Why/Why not?

6 Choose a project

1 Design a poster: Wildlife park or animal centre

1 Imagine you and your group are opening a new park or centre for animals in your area with lots of activities for children and families.

2 Think of a name for your park.

3 Discuss and make a list of the animals that are going to live there.

4 Decide on three special activities for children.

5 Write slogans to attract the interest of visitors.

6 Draw or find pictures of animals that live at your park or centre and stick them on your poster.

7 Display your poster in your classroom.

2 A nature study

1 Find a habitat in or around your school grounds. Habitats can be very small, such as, under a rock, or in a tree or in the pond or even in the grass (if you have a garden you could use that as a habitat to study too.)

2 Spend some time studying this habitat over a number of days and take notes on:
   • The conditions of the habitat.
   • The insects and animals that live there.
   • Find out what they eat and what eats them!
   • Choose one of the insects or animals and draw a picture of it. Label the different parts of its body.

3 Present your findings to the class.

Reflect on your learning

What lessons can we learn from the animal kingdom?

1 Write the name of two animals which live in each habitat.

forest Antarctic grassland mountain

freshwater ocean desert

2 Draw a diagram to illustrate a food chain in one of these habitats.

3 What is a primary consumer? What is a secondary consumer?

4 What characteristics does a tiger have? Write a short description.

5 Give an example of how an animal adapts to its environment.

6 Use these verbs to explain how to care for a cat.

should   must   need to   have to

7 Write a slogan to interest children about the new chicks at the children's farm.

L👀k what I can do!

Write or show examples in your notebook.

1 I can talk about animal habitats and the animals that live there.
2 I can understand diagrams about food chains.
3 I can read and understand a text about animal camouflage.
4 I can talk about how to care for a pet.
5 I can write a leaflet advertising a children's farm.
6 I can read and understand a poem about pets.

Review 5

In pairs, do the tasks in each box. How many points can you get?

1
Write down four adjectives we use to describe personality. Act out four of the adjectives. Can your partner guess what they are?

Total: 8 points

2
Write down three illnesses. Ask your partner, *What's the matter?* Your partner acts out the illness for you to guess.

Total: 6 points

3
Name two adjectives to describe a city and two to describe the country. Take turns to compare the city and the country using the adjectives you have thought of.

Total: 8 points

4
Write down four things you either wear, eat or do during a celebration. Define each one using: **who**, **that** or **which**.

Total: 8 points

5
Name as many jobs you can think of in a minute. Which ones are your favourite jobs? Why?

1 point for each

6
Tell your partner about your last holiday or school trip. Use three verbs in the past simple and two in the past continuous.

Total: 5 points

7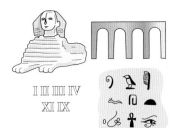
Tell your partner what you can see in these pictures and what each one was used for. Use, **I think**, **I know**, **I believe**.

Total: 8 points

8
Prepare a weather report for tomorrow's weather. Describe the weather in the morning, the afternoon and the evening. Use **will** and adverbs of degree.

Total: 6 points

9
Give advice on how to look after a pet of your choice. Use **should**.

1 point for each

10
Write five quiz questions for your partner about types of animals, their characteristics, their habitats and what they eat.

Name a small animal with long ears that lives in fields.
Total: 10 points

Acknowledgements

The authors and publishers would like to thank the following for their contribution to the development of Stage 5:
Series Editor: Kathryn Harper; Development Editor: Emma Szlachta; Reviewers: Liam Egan, MSc in TESOL; Lois Hopkins, MA Publishing; Ana Pérez Moreno, Licentiate in English Language and in Education; Claire Olmez, BEd, MA ELT; Mary Spratt; Graham Wilson.

Cover artwork: Bill Bolton

The authors and publishers acknowledge the following sources of copyright material and are grateful for the permissions granted. While every effort has been made, it has not always been possible to identify the sources of all the material used, or to trace all copyright holders. If any omissions are brought to our notice, we will be happy to include the appropriate acknowledgements on reprinting.

Text
p. 14 'Our Teacher's Multitalented' copyright © 2004 Kenn Nesbitt, from *When the Teacher isn't Looking,* Meadowbrook Press; p. 14 'Super Samson Simpson' text copyright © 1990 by Jack Prelutsky. Used by permissions of HarperCollins Publishers; p. 28 adapted from the story 'Stone Soup' from ww.bry-backmanor.org; p. 44 'The Lost City' by Margo Fallis, used and adapted with permission of the author; p. 58 *Horrid Henry's Birthday Party* originally appeared in *Horrid Henry and the Secret Club* by Francesca Simon, published by Orion Children's Books, and imprint of the Orion Book Group, London. Text © Francesca Simon 1995, illustrations © Tony Ross 2009; p. 74 excerpt from *The Stowaway* by Karen Hesse, reprinted with the permission of Margaret K. McElderry Books, an imprint of Simon & Schuster Children's Publishing Division. Copyright © 2000 Karen Hesse; p. 86 'Feathers into the wind' from The Story Museum website (www.storymuseum.org.uk/1001 stories) Story told by Chris Smith, written text by Adam Guillain. Crown copyright; p. 88 'The Lambton Worm' used with permission on Paul Perro, www.history-for-kids.com; p. 104 excerpt from *There's a Pharaoh in our Bath!* by Jeremy Strong, Puffin Books, Penguin, by permission of David Higham; p. 118 'A visit from Mr Tree Frog' and p. 120 'If I were a sloth' by Kathy Paysen, from her Rainbows in the Rainforest Collection; p. 134 'My mum won't let me keep a rabbit' by Brian Pattern, from *Gargling with Jelly,* Puffin Books, 1986, reproduced by permission of Penguin Books Ltd, copyright © 1985 and reproduced by permission of the author c/o Rogers, Coleridge & White Ltd, 20 Powis Mews, London W11 1JN.

Photographs
p9 Roger Weber / Photodisc / Thinkstock; p10 Kali Nine LLC / iStock; p11 katkov / iStock / Thinkstock; p12 Sylvain Cazenave / Corbis; p13 Kate Gerson / iStock / Thinkstock; p16 thelefty / Shutterstock; p21 Jochen Tack / Alamy; p22 t Henrik_L / iStock / Thinkstock, b Liba Taylor / Alamy; p23 Jake Lyell / Water Aid / Alamy; p24 ginosphotos / iStock / Thinkstock; p33 Henrik_L / iStock / Thinkstock; p34 l Gabe Palmer / Hemera / Thinkstock, r Jani Bryson / iStock / Thinkstock; p36 t pcruciatti / Shutterstock, b Victor Torres / Shutterstock; p37 l MOF / iStock / Thinkstock, r Barry Mason / Alamy; p38 t James Lee / iStock / Thinkstock, c Chris H. Galbraith / Shutterstock, b Lee Priince / Shutterstock; p40 l Mary Evans Picture Library / Alamy, r Robert Harding World Imagery / Alamy; p41 t John Phillips / UK Press via Getty Images, c AF archive / Alamy, b AF archive / Alamy; p43 AF archive / Alamy; p47 Rampersad Ramautar / iStock / Thinkstock; p50 a Mikadun / Shutterstock, b Skynetphoto / Shutterstock, c David Fowler / Shutterstock; p51 l Fuse / Thinkstock, r Megapress / Alamy; p52 t Migel / Shutterstock, b Valeriy Tretyakov / iStock / Thinkstock; p55 Elena Schweitzer / Thinkstock; p56 gilaxia / iStock; p62 amana images / Thinkstock; p63 Skynetphoto / Shutterstockk; p66 1 © North Wind Picture Archives / Alamy, 2 migstock / Alamy, 3 SuperStock / Getty Images, 4 Lebrecht Music and Arts Photo Library / Alamy, 5 Ewing Galloway / Alamy, 6 ZUMA Press, Inc. / Alamy; p67 l Pictorial Press Ltd / Alamy, c Jamal Saidi / Reuters / Corbis, tr Haruyoshi Yamaguchi / Corbis, br ZUMA Press, Inc.

/ Alamy; p68 t Muir Vidler / Corbis Outline, b Jeff Schultes / Shutterstock.com; p69 Jeff Schultes / Shutterstock.com; p70 l BRUCE COLEMAN INC. / Alamy, r AFP / Getty Images; p72 t © dpa picture alliance / Alamy, b Red Bull Stratos / Red Bull Content Pool / © Red Bull Media House Used with kind permission; p75 Pictorial Press Ltd / Alamy; p79 t Muir Vidler / Corbis Outline, c Red Bull Stratos / Red Bull Content Pool / © Red Bull Media House Used with kind permission, b Pictorial Press Ltd / Alamy; p95 Horizons WWP / Alamy; p96 a Dan Breckwoldt / iStockphoto / Thinkstock, b Purestock / Thinkstock, c x-drew / iStockphoto / Thinkstock, d LianeM / iStockphoto / Thinkstock; p98 t mfron / iStockphoto / Thinkstock, b © Steve Vidler / Alamy; p107 zakazpc / iStock / Thinkstock; p110 background, Andrew McConnell / Alamy; p110 tl Ron Chapple Studios / Thinkstock, tc tockbyte / Thinkstock, tr © Stocktrek Images / Thinkstock, bl © Asianet-Pakistan / Shutterstock, bc Andrew McConnell / Alamy, br Irina Igumnova / iStock / Thinkstock; p111 Stockbyte / Thinkstock; p112 background, © Digital Vision / Thinkstock, p112 t-b © Digital Vision / Thinkstock, Brandon Alms / iStockphoto / Thinkstock, Andrius Gruzdaitis / iStock / Thinkstock, yotrak / Shutterstock; p115 Irina Igumnova / iStock / Thinkstock; p116 holbox / Shutterstock; p117 t shane partridge / iStock / Thinkstock, c Dawn Anderson / iStock / Thinkstock, b ktsimageThinkstock; p123 © Digital Vision / Thinkstock; p125 Dr Morley Reead / Shutterstock; p126 background Tamara Nicol / hemera / Thinkstock; p126 1 Eric Isselée / iStockphoto / Thinkstock, 2 Eric Isselée / Hemera / Thinkstock, 3 frank parker / iStockphoto / Thinkstock, 4 Vladimír Vítek / iStockphoto / Thinkstock, 5 Alessandro Mancini / Alamy, 6 John Pitcher / iStockphoto / Thinkstock, 7 Fuse / Thinkstock, a Aleksander Bolbo / iStock / Thinkstock, b fivepointsix / iStockphoto / Thinkstock, c Tamara Nicol / hemera / Thinkstock, d Steve Henwood / iStockphoto / Thinkstock, e vencavolrab / iStockphoto / Thinkstock, f Stanislav_Moroz / iStockphoto / Thinkstock, g wrangel / iStockphoto / Thinkstock; p128 background, Henrik Larsson / iStockphoto / Thinkstock, p128 t © Ingram Publishing / Thinkstock, c Henrik Larsson / iStockphoto / Thinkstock, b © Zoonar / Thinkstock; p130 l-r Alberto Fabiani / iStock / Thinkstock, Ana Blazic / 3bugsmom / Getty Images / Thinkstock, Jani Bryson / iStock / Thinkstock, a Birute Vijeikiene / iStockphoto / Thinkstock, b songphon / iStockphoto / Thinkstock, c Gelpi / iStockphoto / Thinkstock; p132 l t-b Terry Wilson / iStock, tratong / iStock, Lokibaho / iStock, Jaren Jai Wicklund / Shutterstock, r amattel / iStock; p136 Joshua Lewis / iStockphoto / Thinkstock; p139 t Stanislav_Moroz / iStockphoto / Thinkstock, b Vladimír Vítek / iStockphoto / Thinkstock.

Key: t = top, c = centre, b = bottom, l = left, r = right.

Development of this publication has made use of the Cambridge English Corpus (CEC). The CEC is a multi-billion word computer database of contemporary spoken and written English. It includes British English, American English and other varieties of English. It also includes the Cambridge Learner Corpus, developed in collaboration with Cambridge English Language Assessment. Cambridge University Press has built up the CEC to provide evidence about language use that helps to produce better language teaching materials.

This product is informed by the English Vocabulary Profile, built as part of English Profile, a collaborative programme designed to enhance the learning, teaching and assessment of English worldwide. Its main funding partners are Cambridge University Press and Cambridge English Language Assessment and its aim is to create a 'profile' for English linked to the Common European Framework of Reference for Languages (CEFR). English Profile outcomes, such as the English Vocabulary Profile, will provide detailed information about the language that learners can be expected to demonstrate at each CEFR level, offering a clear benchmark for learners' proficiency. For more information, please visit www.englishprofile.org